PRAISE FOR *I'LL TI*

"Written with the immediacy of the present and the wisdom of the intervening decades, *I'll Tell You a Secret* is a perceptive meditation on the thrall of infatuation."

— Sandra Martin, *Globe and Mail*

"Expressive, lyric and beautifully paced."

— Jury citation, Governor General's Awards

"Coleman's present-tense narrative story captures the immediacy and visceral force of adolescence, and holds that spell throughout. She conjures the spirit of an intellectually aware but inexperienced girl, with all her wilfulness, doubts and insecurities — as well as a strength that pushes her beyond her fears."

— *McGill News*

"The truth conveyed in the book is emotional, subjective, and one-sided, echoing Alice Munro's stories of girlhood in their narrowness of location and point of view, as well as their concern with what is unspoken and unrealized."

— *Quill & Quire*

"Though Hugh MacLennan couldn't save her personal life, he did posthumously inspire a great book. With a few sparse scenes exquisitely rendered, Coleman . . . sets character and circumstance in collision mode and stays the course."

— Montreal *Gazette*

I'LL TELL YOU
A SECRET

A MEMORY OF SEVEN SUMMERS

ANNE COLEMAN

M&S

Library and Archives Canada Cataloguing in Publication

Coleman, Anne, 1936-
I'll tell you a secret : a memory of seven summers / Anne Coleman.

ISBN 0-7710-2278-6 (bound).— ISBN 0-7710-2279-4 (pbk.)

1. College teachers – Canada – Biography.   2. Coleman, Anne, 1936-
– Childhood and youth.   3. MacLennan, Hugh, 1907-1990 – Friends and
associates.   4. North Hatley (Québec) – Biography.   I. Title.

PR55.C65A3 2004   C818'.603   C2004-902519-8

We acknowledge the financial support of the Government of Canada through
the Book Publishing Industry Development Program and that of the
Government of Ontario through the Ontario Media Development
Corporation's Ontario Book Initiative. We further acknowledge the
support of the Canada Council for the Arts and the Ontario Arts Council
for our publishing program.

Typeset in Centaur by M&S, Toronto
Printed and bound in Canada

This book is printed on acid-free paper that is 100% recycled,
ancient-forest friendly (40% post-consumer recycled).

McClelland & Stewart Ltd.
The Canadian Publishers
481 University Avenue
Toronto, Ontario
M5G 2E9
www.mcclelland.com

1 2 3 4 5   09 08 07 06 05

In memory of
Mr. MacLennan
Omnia mutantur, nihil interit

and for

my children, Paul and Jane
my seven grandchildren
my sister Carol, my brother, Charles

I'll Tell You
a Secret

EARLY ONE MORNING

1950

I am swimming up into the morning through green-gold water that is shot with sunrays as I surface. It is a dream and I float out of the image as I open my eyes.

And I am in my own bed. I am lying on my smooth white sheet, my covers on the floor, and I can hear a wild tumult of birdsong: the trees, even the verandah vine, are full of so many birds singing that it is amazing that everyone isn't awake, but all the sounds are outside. Within the house all is quiet and everyone still sleeps.

I lean up on my elbow to look through my wide open window. The air is cool but the day will be warm, maybe even hot.

I hitch myself up to look out and better see my maple tree, which is at this moment seething with the singing birds. It is

huge and ancient and because of the way the lawn slopes below
the house, I am almost on a level with its crown. The leaves
nearest me are in shadow and the sun is lighting the ones only
at the very top on the eastern side. The sunlit ones are the
bright new green of early summer. Below me the grass is dark
green, still wet with dew. I know just how it would feel, cold,
under my feet and that I would leave silver tracks. By my new
watch I see that it is six o'clock.

I will think about my secret.

I rest my arms on the sill and notice how brown they
already are, making the little blond hairs on them look white
as they catch the light. I am wearing pale orange pajamas,
short-sleeved, many times washed, in fact a faint peach colour
now, and rather shrunken. Or is it that I am now so tall? My
arms and legs have lengthened even since Christmas.

At every time of year my first ritual on waking, when I am
home, is to study the leaves and bark of my maple. I know
from their look how early it is; also in the evenings, how late.
I am not someone who really needs a watch but time is important to me and I like to be precise. And I like my watch, which
is a man's and what I asked for. On long summer evenings, I
stare at the leaves until the shadows have gathered and deep-
ened and then it is important that I sleep at once. I must not
still be awake when darkness overtakes the tree.

From the tree, I also know the weather and the tempera-
ture: in winter the tree's unprotected skin pales, becomes dry

and brittle, grey with the cold. Watching from my window, I know how it would feel under my hand. And it darkens with warmth and moisture on a milder day while the snow around its base greys and coarsens. In spring the bark is a richer brown and I watch the thin, high branches, the fragile black twigs against the sky, and think of the sap mounting. My brother and I pound in sharp spigots, one to each side to hang a pail on, and tap it. The sap tastes of spring, thin and green. We boil it down and make a tiny jug of syrup.

I am obsessed with seasons as well as time. I am a very odd child, according to my sisters. Even though I am a quiet person, it seems that I am turning out to be the most extreme member of the family, in some ways anyway. I am not sure how much choice a person has in who she turns out to be. The difficulty is in wanting the things and being the ways other people expect. A person can make herself do certain things perhaps, but she can't make herself want to. In my case I don't even make myself do them.

The situation is getting worse because I am about to be fourteen. Increasingly I feel the push of other people's expectations on me of what a girl is supposed to be and I can't want any of the things I'm supposed to be eager for. My sisters have gone ahead of me along the path into, and in the case of my older sister, out the other side of, adolescence. They have had to endure miseries and perils, and I have watched in dread the tortures of shyness and holding back in the case of one, and the worrying but brave ventures forth in the case of the other, both of them being determined, throughout, to succeed at being the right sort of woman whatever the cost. The miseries and perils were about having the wrong sort of hair (we all have curly) and having in every way to look and behave unnaturally or face terrible scorn. I long to bypass the whole stage and I will, somehow. I don't seem able to do anything else, in fact.

However, at the moment I am so happy I can't even worry. I am home from boarding school and I will never go back there. Mother has promised. We may even move back to Toronto and I'd go to school there. I have been home for two weeks, but still each morning I wake up to joy and relief at being in my own bed. And there is my new and secret friendship. It makes me feel a little bit excited all the time, even when I am doing other things.

My grandmother is visiting, and my aunt, who lives with her. This is their summer holiday in the country and they are here for three weeks.

My grandmother has always worn a girdle and stays. When I was a smaller girl, I would sit on her bed and watch her get dressed. It was a long and complicated matter. She had to deal with several layers, while more or less lying down against the pillows. The room was dim because her window had an awning to keep out the sun, and that made her tasks all the more mysterious. While still in her loose summer dressing gown, she would begin. The first step was using a big peach-coloured puff to smooth talcum powder over herself, slipping her hands under her gown to do this. She never would be fully undressed in front of me. Then she would place tiny, flattish pink powder-puffs in strategic, tender spots against her pink plumpness (of which I would have some glimpses) to protect her soft skin from the bones of her stays, or girdle. This at first flapped hugely wide and spoked, and then was heaved firmly into position — an uncomfortable moment requiring an indrawn breath — and then hooked and laced. I remember how I would sit there, grasping my bony knees tightly, watching her body that seemed to have no bones at all.

Her drawers were heavy silk and had legs. They were oyster coloured, or deep cream. I planned, and still plan, never to wear anything but cotton myself, no matter how old I get. I will never wear anything that could be called "drawers." Not that I can imagine getting old, not me. A slip next. Then garters, with more powder-puffs carefully placed to protect the soft, dimply skin of her thighs.

I always wear as few clothes as possible in summer.

And I have always planned to take my body entirely for granted.

But the fact of the matter is that my own body is changing. No one else is noticing, but it is.

Enough. I bounce my fists on the sill. And jump lightly off the bed, as I don't want to wake anybody else up, not for their sake but for my own. I peel off my pajamas and thrust my legs into my shorts that still hold my underpants from yesterday and I stand for a moment looking down at my new, small breasts. I like them. They are interesting. And they feel interesting. There is a sort of firm disk inside them that is changing and softening and they are getting bigger. The funny thing is, and I know it may not be logical, but I feel that the changes in my body have no relation to, are in no way like, the changes that must have happened to other women in my family. They are entirely private and mine and will not make me a woman like any of them.

I pull on a crumpled cotton blouse. It has been mashed against the cushion on my chair under the heavy book I am reading and that I threw there last night. I snatch up the book and run silently downstairs in my bare feet.

No one else gets up until about seven-thirty, not even my younger brother. The kitchen has a large bay window but it faces west and so the room is cool and shadowy now though by lunchtime it will be full of sunlight. I pour cereal into a bowl and add brown sugar, no milk, and I take three of the early plums and rearrange the bowl so no one will notice that I take more than is fair.

The verandah extends almost the full length of the house at the front and there is a Dutchman's pipe vine that climbs all the posts and runs along the edge of the roof. As well, it has almost filled in the eastern end of the verandah where we have an old porch glider. That is where I lie on my stomach, propped on my elbows, in a dapple of sunshine. The leaves of the vine are large and round and a light bright green. Without looking directly at them, I am also aware of the two tall elms at the eastern edge of the lawn and I can see the three birch trees below our road that slightly screen the Bassetts' cottage. Their lawn runs down to the lakeside road and then there is the lake itself, glinting here and there through the trees.

I am perfectly safe and no one can spring forth and mock me, as could happen so suddenly at boarding school if I ever let down my guard. I love knowing that. The birds are still singing though not quite as loudly. I eat a plum first. The thin, tough skin snaps under my teeth and a drop of juice falls onto the cover of my book. I lick it up.

I open my book and start to eat my cereal with my fingers. I am rereading *War and Peace*, in the translation by Constance Garnett. Is that a man or a woman? I always mean to ask someone and never do. And how would "Constance" be a man, anyway? Maybe it's the full form of the name: I am used to "Connies." And a strong quality like constance could be a man's or a woman's, couldn't it? Or maybe I mistrust the notion of a woman doing something so wonderful and huge as translating *War and Peace* from the Russian. But I plan to learn Russian one day and would like to know of a woman who did manage it, and how and where she did so. I am in love with Prince André. The little Princess is dead and all should be plain sailing for him and Natasha. I fear and hate Anatole and dread what is coming.

Mr. MacLennan will know if "Constance" is a man or a woman. I will ask him today maybe, if I get a chance. I like to have a question to greet him with.

I rest my chin on my hands for a minute and think of Mr. MacLennan. I never think of him by his first name and don't really even want to be asked ever to use it. It is like Jane and Mr. Rochester. It would be much more thrilling had she continued to call him that even after their marriage, the marriage that happens when he is so tamed, even maimed, and has become just "Edward." All the excitement has leaked out of the situation by then.

Mr. MacLennan's eyes are bright blue and they sort of narrow and glint when I come along, because of the way his cheeks go when he smiles. He has a distinctive smile, his mouth curving up at the sides the way a child draws a smile and the way people's faces mostly don't go. I love the way he smiles. He is an extremely handsome man, especially of course his legs. I think "of course" because we have made a thing in our family, my sisters and I that is, about his legs. It started before he and I became friends and now I don't particularly like it that they still comment on his wonderful legs when I consider him to be mine. However, I have to contend with it because they don't know that we are friends and I don't want them to.

I've finished the cereal, and the sugar alone lines the bottom of the bowl. I lean over and use my tongue to catch every morsel and eat it. This is the kind of thing that drives my sisters to despair of me, as would my still unbrushed hair, which falls in a curly tousle down my back. Actually my mother often helps me evade their scorn and I hear her now in the kitchen. She'll brush my hair for me as I sit on the stool. She likes it that I am still, at moments, what she can consider "a little girl" and that my hair is her responsibility.

At school I had no idea how to wash and braid my own hair. The shame and worry of it was excruciating as it got heavier and dirtier. And the desperate attempts to do it in a tiny, cracked basin with a hard cake of soap that didn't smell nice. And then the utter impossibility of getting that soap, so thick and greasy-feeling, gummy, out of the huge mass of wet hair.

I am a contradiction even to myself. And Mother has bemoaned the fact: "Anne, my darling, how can you be so vague and helpless?" she has said to me, and often too, or something of the same sort. Yesterday she was on about it again: "I simply cannot understand how it can be! I see you sailing your boat on the windiest day. I watched you on Saturday and it was so wild no one else would even leave the shore, and there you were, looking so calm and competent I couldn't believe it. And your canoeing last summer, all those silver spoons you won, and the cup. Those are practical skills too! You do some things so well —" and she looked at me, "and about other things you are impossibly incompetent!" I know what she means. The different parts of me don't fit together to make a sensible picture of a person.

"I think you just don't care about some things," Mother said. "But you should. It's time for you to care. It would make life simpler for you." She even sighed at that point which made me feel sorry for being such a difficult daughter, and also guilty because she wasn't really angry, just puzzled, as I am myself. But it has to be my fault and I actually deserve to be chastised. "Other people can't understand," she went on. "I don't think they understood at school — how you could be so good at some things. I was very proud of you when Miss Gillard told me at the Closing how well you'd done in your mathematics. But then you are so hopeless at other ordinary tasks. I'm afraid they think you're doing it on purpose to annoy."

Mother is always trying to bolster my confidence, I can see that, mentioning my good points. She is on my side, but we are both baffled because it's true there are a lot of things I can do. Despite being so homesick and unhappy, I had really high marks. But then I'd run up against some simple thing I couldn't do properly and I'd get defensive because I was ashamed, I suppose, even though I didn't actually want to do whatever it was. And often had no intention of trying. I hated when the matron threw her hands in the air in fury and what seemed to be real contempt because I couldn't wash my hair. Plus, I couldn't thread a sewing machine, and never could master it in the face of her anger. She hated me. But that didn't make me change, I'm afraid. Doing something because someone is angry doesn't seem to me to be a good reason.

Still, how could I have had Mother, and before her, Helen, my nanny, though we never called her that, till I was five, wash my hair thousands of times over my lifetime and never really have noticed how they did the deed?

I sit on the stool with my eyes closed while Mother brushes my hair.

I am thinking of a man who I have just found out is forty-three years old. I read it on the paper jacket of his most recent novel. I already read the book last year but I pulled it from the shelf last night to study his picture. His birthdate was there: 1907, which is the same year Laurence Olivier was born. I fell in love with Laurence Olivier in *Henry V* and *Hamlet*, and I have memorized all his soliloquies. I've read the plays but we also have him doing the main speeches on records; I know exactly all his inflections and can hear his voice in my head. So, two men I love are rather old for me, to say the least, and both are the same age, born in 1907, which is only five years after my own father was born.

It is quite a different matter when it is Mr. MacLennan. With Laurence Olivier, and it's the same with Prince André, the whole thing is obviously total fantasy, a daydream, and even I know I am never going to bump into either of them at the North Hatley Club, even though I have plotted scenes in which that very thing happens. (I am crossing the sand and hear a Voice, the accent English, or Russian, "Who is that lovely young girl, with her long legs and her curly hair?") With Mr. MacLennan it is a different thing because he is real.

I am maybe not a little girl. I am maybe someone he could love back.

I open my eyes and I stare out the window at bright leaves as my mother rhythmically brushes my hair. I am in a sort of trance.

It is late morning and I am beaching my canoe at the Club.

Our boathouse is directly across from the Club and as I paddled I could see the village on my left, the old white houses and the few stores that line the curve of the end of the lake, and the two short bridges, one for cars and one for the train to cross the river where it heads out from the lake. Just before the village there is a small park with a white bandstand in the middle of it. There is a low stone wall along the edge of the water there, where when I was quite small I once fell because I was running so fast along it. A stranger took me back to her house and taped me up, so it was a bit of an adventure, seeing in her house, and having to clench my teeth as she dabbed on iodine, which we didn't use at our house. Across from the park is the small brown-shingled Baptist Church. Our church, the Anglican, is around the curve and up the hill a little way, behind the Connaught Inn. The side of the lake we live on has mostly the big summer cottages, hidden in the trees unless they are right on the water. The lake is nine miles long but it takes a turn so that you can't see all the way down, just the different points. On our side there is Yellow House Point, Hovey Manor Point, Black Point, and Blueberry Point and then you can't see the rest. From Hovey Manor on, there are no houses at all and the forest is extremely dense, also steep, right down to the water, except where there are pebble beaches that we can only get to by boat. We always have my birthday picnic down there. The lake is in a valley, and the hills that make it feel so contained and complete are round and green in summer and in winter vary from day to day depending on the snow. I don't know which season I prefer; each always seems my favourite while it is happening.

The lake is smooth and the sun beats down on the back of my neck. Mother braided my hair and pinned it up for coolness and it makes me feel lighter. She also made me put on clean clothes. She overheard Ruth telling me that I looked a mess. Also that my mouth was much too big and I'd never be pretty. When Ruth had gone back upstairs again, Mother said, "You have your grandmother's mouth, Anne" – I know she means my father's mother – "and she was beautiful." Grandma and Auntie were down by this time and they both nodded in agreement. I never knew that grandmother and am not certain I am reassured. There are only two pictures of her that I ever saw and she looks sad in both of them. I'll have to check again sometime about the beauty. There is a conspiracy of silence about her though that I can never break through and I have no sense of what she can have been like. Now I know I have her mouth. Once before, Mother told me I have her hands. It's a strange feeling, to have bits of a person long-dead alive in my body. I look down at my narrow hands; they are much stronger than they look. The nails are bitten, a habit I cannot break even when offered bribes to do so.

Now, I walk across the hot sand and step up onto the verandah. Because I turn fourteen later this very week, on July sixth, I consider I can use the grown-ups' porch. Anyone under fourteen must not set a toe on it, as it is the preserve of adults, though that law is especially strict three times a week when a lot of old ladies appear and sit and drink tea and eat little sandwiches and cakes and watch everyone. They dress up for these teas in summer silk or lawn dresses, often white with blue flowers, or navy with white flowers, a kind of dress favoured by Grandma, though Grandma never comes to these teas, perhaps because all the other women have been at the Club forever and as she did not have her childhood summers in North Hatley, she could never be one of them. They wear the same sort of heavy stockings she does and laced, old-lady, white summer shoes and are really exactly like her, on the surface anyway, but she would still be an outsider. She is very much an insider in her own town (Buckingham, Quebec), so she leaves it at that, I guess. It may also be that as a minister's widow, even though he was a canon, which is some sort of slightly better-than-the-usual kind of clergyman, Grandma is not a rich old lady. Actually she would have been rich, had her brothers, also all Anglican ministers, not tricked her out of her inheritance long ago, another murky and mostly closed chapter in our family history, although my father has given us some details about it. It is his own family secrets he won't speak of at all. The old Club women get even more dressed up when they come to watch the dances, which are in the ballroom, the large room where the children play during the day if it's too hot outside or when it's raining. The old ladies never dance themselves but they watch keenly.

No one notices me at the Club as I sit in the shadow on the wide railing but I am going to be a writer and I take note of all the tales. Everyone's family is interconnected with everyone else's and there are scandals and grudges, also jokes, that go back generations. Mostly they are surprisingly good-natured about old grievances and evil deeds. There are not such dark corners of unacceptable mysteries as there are in my family.

Two women are talking. They are sisters-in-law and about the same age as my mother. One is beautiful and wears very bright lipstick. She also plucks her eyebrows into perfect arches that make her look surprised, though she is far from surprised, I think. I consider her to be quite a cynical woman. The other is very down-to-earth and I like her and often crew for her in sailing races, or for her son who is my age and with whom I have a rather non-talking friendship. They are speaking about the fact that they are both having babies after a long gap – their other children are all around my age. The beautiful one – and she is still beautiful despite her stomach being all swollen as the rest of her is as slim as ever – she says, "Well, I finally agreed to do it," and she laughs a laugh that has a sharp edge to it. I study her face and see her eyes narrow in a way she can't realize spoils her beauty as does her pursing her lips. Calculating, that's what she looks right now. "He insisted and insisted and would not shut up. God, it was getting to be a huge thing with him – and I made a bargain. I'd do one last baby – and, for my trouble – a trip to Europe this fall, when I've popped, and a new mink coat. Full-length too." She laughs again. "But what a bore!" She slaps her round, taut stomach in a way that makes me wince. It looks a bit mean to the baby inside and even to her own self. Her sister-in-law doesn't respond to this goading. It's her brother who will be stumping up for the trip and the coat; I can tell she almost says something back. I know she feels entirely differently about her own late baby. Both women seem quite old to me to be having babies, but I don't know how old a woman can be and still be able to have one. But the nicer one told me one day when we were in her boat that she feels incredibly lucky, really thrilled.

Club people, as far as I can tell, live only in their own group of Club members. It's as if the rest of the village is invisible to them, except for the fact that village people open the summer people's cottages and clean for them and do their laundry and their lawns. But it's still the way it is in novels set in an earlier time: if only a servant is in the room, no one is there. No English person, Club or not, has any truck with the French people who live down the Capelton Road. That's a road that leads off from the Baptist Church and winds along the river. The houses down there are different from the summer cottages, many being very small and shackish. There is a lot of variety in this village even though it is small. To me, it is like a rambling house in which there seem to any ordinary observer to be no connections between the rooms. But actually it is like my Aunt Fanny's house in Buckingham where there are little doors at the back of cupboards so you can slip from one room to another without going into the hall. But in the case of North Hatley, there is no hall. I think there are only a few people who know of the little passages that link the rooms. I am one of them. For example, I know that there are two real-life "first Mrs. Rochesters" hidden in this village.

Most of the Club members are Americans. There are stories that often get told of the old days when these families, all from the Scarlett O'Hara South, would come up in their private railroad cars and would keep the blinds pulled carefully down as they travelled through the northern States. What would happen if they looked out and saw enemy people or even enemy fields and towns? Would they faint with horror and rage? Once across the border into Quebec they could snap up the blinds and look out. Many of the North Hatley cottages are very large, though fairly shabby sometimes, and they have servants' wings that are shut off behind doors covered with a kind of dark green felt; I suppose so that any noise of servants' toil or even conversation can't disturb the real family. Some people still bring their black servants with them. Across the road from us is an old American general from some long-ago war. He has a uniformed chauffeur who is always out polishing the car. Despite the uniform and his handsomeness in it, he is just a member of the Kezar family in the village and the general's cook is local too. The chauffeur's first name is Royce, which is what Uncle Bunny would call "an expensive name" – meaning that it is rather an uppity one for the person's circumstances. But it fits perfectly with this job he has, working for a rich American general, in a way his parents could not possibly have foreseen. I like that.

Last summer I had a friend, Bill, who was staying with his grandmother in one of those cottages, not at all a shabby one, quite a grand one, and huge. He was a year older than I and his grandmother had given him a little outboard motorboat in which we went out every day and fished. We'd go way down the lake and often stay all day, and cook our little bass and perch over a fire we'd make, and then putt-putt home after supper. He was a tall, thin, serious boy with a nice face and smooth light brown hair and, like the boy I sail with, he didn't say much. We only talked about what we were doing and I never knew exactly why only he and his grandmother and her fat black chauffeur and her thin black cook were living in that great big place all summer. The only clue was a lie – why he had to tell it. But I don't know which of the statements he made was actually the lie: he told me his mother was away in Europe, and then when Jean, another friend of mine who came along with us one day, mentioned that her mother was dead, Bill said his was too. So which was the truth? I had a feeling something else entirely was true, that she had gone off with another man. I'll probably not ever find out and he's not back this summer.

The reason I am at the Club this morning is that when my brother, Chuck, and I collected the mail at the Post Office for Mother, I saw Mr. MacLennan on the tennis courts, which are right there beside the Post Office. I went along to the library too, which meant I had to pass right by the courts, but I'm not sure if he saw me. He has to win no matter what — or that's how he seems to play anyway — so that he can't really look to the sides. I collected two more books by Erich Maria Remarque: *Three Comrades*, which I haven't read, and *All Quiet on the Western Front*, which I have. They are extremely sad and really give the feelings, not just the facts, of what war is like, for Germans too, who are ordinary young men not so different from the men on our side. Of course it was the First World War, not the Second. I need to have these books waiting for when I finish *War and Peace* again. I always have to have fresh books ready. It's dreadful when I run out. That was the worst thing about King's Hall, or one of the worst (I haven't decided which aspect of that school was the most horrible, but maybe I don't have to now) was that there were hardly any good books. Really none, as any that looked as if they might be possible turned out not to be. Not that there was any privacy to read in.

I figure that Mr. MacLennan will finish playing just before noon and he might just come down to the Clubhouse after.

I didn't instantly think he was so marvellous, two years ago when I was first aware of him. He was just another grown-up who we would all watch, my sisters and I, and no more interesting than several others. It's only in the last ten days that he's started really to be my friend. I'm not sure what happened, what changed him. I'm not even sure what changed from my point of view, though it happened to me first.

The first time I remember noticing him was when our house was being redone, the summer I was twelve. Mother couldn't make our meals in the kitchen because for weeks and weeks it was all taken apart, and so we went over to the boarding house, Leducs', for our dinners. Leducs' is on the same side of the lake as our house, so we just had to walk to the end of our road and then a little way along a path, and through some woods and past "Snake Town," a pile of boards and logs named that by Chuck for the snakes that inhabited it and that always startled me, even when I half-expected to see them. (I never get used to snakes.)

I liked the walk over there, even the worry about the snakes, and the anticipation of what lay ahead, which was the interesting people-watching. Once we entered the dining room – and the house must have been specially built as a boarding house as it was so large – it was as if we had stepped onto a stage. The six of us would sit down at our table, which was the longest one and in the middle, and we would be at once in the centre of an unfolding drama, many dramas really. Each of the tables around us would soon be filled by summer people, most of them at that time unknown to us, because even though we'd been coming to North Hatley forever and our father had come as a child too, we had only just that summer joined the Club. These were all Club people. For years my father resisted our joining. It was for snobs: there was a feeling of that. Also, though, I have a sense that he just resists joining anything. He's someone on the outside of things, like me. Maybe he wishes he weren't like that? I don't have a deep understanding of my father, even though we are alike. Many of the Club people came up from the States, or some of them from Montreal or Toronto, and I guess they didn't want the bother of cooking or had been unable to find someone to cook for them at their cottages, and so here they were, night after night, having their not-at-all fancy but not bad dinners.

We watched them come in and cross the room to their tables, always the same ones. We watched how they interacted or mainly didn't with those at other tables; they all knew each other but apart from greetings on arrival, fluting, gushing, or gruff depending on their role, they did not talk among themselves. There rarely was any chatting from table to table. We were enormously intrigued by them as they were all so distinctive, some glamorous: even just to come over to Leducs' these ones got dressed up; some were eccentrically casual. We had names for them: the Perfect Man, thin and stiff like a wooden boy doll with his patent-leather hair and pointed profile; the Pretty Lady, who looked just like the actress Margaret Leighton, according to Mother, and who had the husband with the strangely shaped head (extra-packed full of brains, we figured

— he was a professor) and the grown-up son unfortunately just like his father. There were a couple of elderly single women. They were the most eccentric of all but in imposing not pathetic ways and they read their books throughout the meal, looking up now and again over their glasses. There were no other really young people. When we did learn the real names, we discovered that Club people, especially the Americans, often had first names fitting Uncle Bunny's definition of expensive ones, like Sumner, Pennington, Page, de Wolfe, and Franklin. One of the elderly women was even called Eloise.

It was at Leducs' where I first saw Mr. MacLennan and it's funny to remember this, given how I feel about him now, but we used to laugh at him a bit. He would come through the curtains that framed the entrance and were one of the reasons the room seemed so stage-like, and he would throw back his head, and his gaze would sweep the room in a godly manner. I'm afraid my sister Carol and I used to do imitations of this arrival of his if we ever got there before everyone else and the coast was clear: the hands back and to the sides holding the curtains, the gaze. Did he even bow a little to the seated mortals or did we make that part up? His wife would be there too but I prefer not to think about her now. Of course back then, before I cared about him, I would giggle with Carol at what an unmatched pair they were, she much older-looking and so homely.

There was also his voice. He has the sort of English accent which always makes my father's face assume a particular expression, if the person is as Canadian as we are and doing it on purpose. I'd rather not think about that.

But then last summer, when I saw him more at the Club, dressed for tennis, and I watched him play, and also read his novels and realized that not only was he well known but he was also a good writer, and since that's what I've always planned to be, I started to see him differently.

This intensified last summer. I thought he looked so marvellous that, somehow, I could hardly see him. He held his head in a way that I know is arrogant but that I now like, and his tennis whites showed off his brown arms and those legs my sisters go on about. The effect was so dazzling I could hardly take it in. I've thought about that dazzle since. I think when you first adore someone it's as if they are surrounded by rays of light that almost make it impossible to look, and that no one else notices of course. It made me speculate about the halos the artists paint around Jesus and Mary: the dazzle comes from the sheer excitement inside the person watching. So that was the way it was until ten days ago.

On that day – it was a Monday – I was walking along the dirt road that passes his cottage. He lives on the highest of the roads that run parallel to the lake. All the roads are unpaved and casual. The rain makes shallow holes in them and they are a bit bumpy to drive along. They are bordered by trees, with

daisies and day lilies and milkweed in the ditches. The cottages
are not the most grand ones but are still quite big and nice old
shingled places, some just brown, some painted white. His is
white. I had just been walking across the pasture and thought I
would go home the long way, down past the ballpark and along
the lake. I make up reasons that aren't entirely to do with the
main reason — to see if he might be on his verandah or in his
garden — but aren't exactly lies to myself, either, as I would go
this way often even if he was away, which he sometimes is.

He was on his verandah. I gave a very quick glance and
could see his outline behind the screen but he might not have
been looking out. I walked on without slowing at all and soon
was past his cottage and on my way to the ballpark hill. My
heart beats fast when I am near him now, even when I am just
near his house and he might be inside. It had just calmed down
to normal when I heard his car door slam. I knew it had to be
him as there was no other car parked there that day. He started
it and came slowly along behind me. And stopped beside me
and his window was open.

"Do you want a ride, Anne?" he said.

He smiled at me. That was the first time I saw, directed at
me, Anne Coleman, that smile.

"You walk like an Indian," he said. "You put your feet down
perfectly straight." I stared into his blue eyes. I was so surprised
that he knew who I was. "And you hold yourself so straight
and yet relaxed. You seem to float along. It's remarkable."

He had studied my walk.

I hadn't even been sure he knew my name, who I was, apart from one of the Coleman girls. Everyone in North Hatley knows who everyone else is, in a general way, but a grown-up wouldn't necessarily know one child in a family from another.

"So, do you want a ride?"

Of course I wanted a ride.

So that was the way it was. I am kind of muddled about it.

I know that I was the one who noticed him, and I know I watched out for him and deliberately walked where he might see me. But all the time, at the same time, I didn't take myself seriously. I never really thought, not really, that he would actually notice me, that he would start looking back. In a certain way, I of course wanted him to but in another it would be too alarming.

I guess I thought I was invisible, in the way that I am to the Club women because I'm just a kid, the way the villagers to them are just "things" almost, that do their work for them. I sit on the railing and listen to the women tell their secrets and they don't think for a minute that I understand what they are talking about or that it matters. So with Mr. MacLennan I was playing a game; it was all make-believe, and he would be no more likely to look at me and talk to me than Laurence Olivier, up on the screen, would be likely to turn away from Jean Simmons, stare out into the darkened theatre and say, "Anne! Hello!" Or Prince André reach a slim but strong, white, and princely hand out of the printed page to take mine.

This all may be untrue. I try to be honest with myself or there is no point in trying to work things out, to understand how people, including me, are. But I am not sure at all if I am even being honest now. Had it been a game? The funny thing is, I don't know.

And now he is talking to me. We've had two quite long conversations, one at the edge of his garden, and one at the Club and I've had two more rides in his car.

I hop down from the verandah railing and cross the sand again. Some kids have swum out to the raft and I see Johnnie Bassett standing on the high-diving tower, balanced on the handgrips so he's as high as he possibly can be and he's waving his arms in the air. He's a white-blond, tanned, very handsome boy, a beautiful boy, and I like him a lot. I wonder why I can see this about him but not get any of those fierce feelings I have for Mr. MacLennan. I watch him spring for a second up onto his toes and then he is in the air, wildly leaping, and then far, far under the water. He rises, spitting, his hair sleeked back, and he is laughing, his eyelashes stuck together in clumps from the water.

I lie on my stomach on the dock and look down into the water. Listening to the lapping, chortling sounds it makes deep underneath the boards.

Did I will him to like me? There is a thing in our family about my will, how I always get what I want. Everyone gets

exasperated with me because no one can make me do what I
don't want to do. This goes back at least to kindergarten when
I was in a school play and then refused to go back for the
second night: I'd done it once so that was that. My mother
had to drag my costume on me and then prise my hands from
around the bedpost and haul me off to the school. I think that
was the last time anyone else ever won. At King's Hall I had
some terrible moments when a mistress would try to force me
to do something — eat liver for the worst example — and I
would not, not in the face of the whole school waiting, unable
to leave their tables until Anne Coleman ate her liver. Teachers
always had to give up on something like that with me though
because I never would. I don't especially want to be this way,
but it's just the way I am.

I told Mr. MacLennan about the liver episode one day
while we were sitting on the Club dock: "You see, everyone in
the whole huge dining room was furious with me. They had
to be silent of course, but I could feel it. Rage was just seething
in that room. They weren't going to have any time before afternoon classes if I didn't get eating fast." He watched me and I
could tell he was amused. "The thing is, I couldn't open my
lips to it. The girl beside me reached across and cut a bit and
put out a wodge of potato with it and tried to push it into me
but there was no way my mouth would allow it in. My lips
were sealed." The mistress who was attempting to force me was
Miss Ramsay and I had liked her, up to that point. She taught

math and I was best at it, maybe in the whole school, and now here she was being cruel and ferocious, as if she'd never put all those ten-out-of-tens with exclamation marks on my papers.

I went on and told the worst bit, that finally she just had to give up. I would never let her win and she knew it. So she told me in a furious and cold voice to take my plate to the kitchen – everyone else's had been cleared by the maids – and then the whole school watched me walk across the room and back, and then she said, "Anne Coleman, your legs are so thin I don't know how you walk on them," and she said it loudly enough so that everyone heard and stared at my legs. It was extremely humiliating. Mr. MacLennan looked down at my legs.

We both looked at them: my right foot was balanced on the big toe of my left. I was in bare feet and about two yards of leg seemed to be exposed. I felt self-conscious suddenly.

"They look just fine to me," he said. And they did look fine, really, long and slim and brown, every bit of them on view because my shorts were so skimpy.

"Well, I've got back to normal now," I said. And it is amazing how swiftly I gained back to normal weight once I was home. Mother has remarked on it several times because I guess she was worried about me. I'm still thin but no longer alarming.

There was another uncomfortable element about Miss Ramsay's cruelty. It's too confusing or embarrassing to explain to Mr. MacLennan. Miss Ramsay herself was crippled, her whole body twisted, her back humped. I couldn't understand how someone who must have always suffered from being deformed could be so unkind about what she saw as a bad physical aspect of someone else, and a child too. Also I felt that I couldn't be angry at her as she had such a disadvantage. Somehow made the whole thing more hurtful because she knew how it felt.

And now here I am, pondering over my feelings for Mr. MacLennan and, even more interesting, his for me.

I really like the way he looks at me when I tell him things.

But I don't understand it. It can't just be my famous strong will because that's to do with refusing to do something. Using my will to make someone else do something is pretty different. As if I could beam a ray at them that would compel them. Surely I can't do that.

The thing is, he really likes me. I can tell.

I don't have to be the one who necessarily looks out for him. He comes to me. He crosses his lawn from where he's gardening, or he comes over to where I am on the dock, at the Club.

We have important conversations. It's rare for me to have a real talk with a grown-up. In fact when I think of it, I never have had what you could call a real conversation with a male person, except for my father and my brother and my Uncle

Bunny. Mostly my friends have been girls, though I have some friends who are boys, like Bill last summer. And there are various other Club boys who come by our dock and take me sailing in their bigger boats, which is fun and sometimes I crew for them in races. And of course there are the Bassetts across the road, and David who lives next door, all of whom I've known forever and am perfectly comfortable to go swimming or sailing with. When we were a bit younger we all played hide-and-seek or tap-the-icebox every night after supper. We still lie around on the living-room floor on rainy days and play cards. But we've never had what I would now call real conversations. That is, conversations about what we are reading (they wouldn't be likely to read what I do for one thing) or what we really think about.

It's quite different with Mr. MacLennan. He asks me questions: "Anne, what are you reading now?" and, "What do you think about it?" or "What do you think he's trying to say through all those descriptions of the trenches? Is he just giving us the scene, is his goal impressionistic, or is there more to it?" Or he may be more pointed in his question and I know he is trying to lead me, which I may resist. "Does he have a theme underneath, do you think?" And I'll know he thinks there is one and I may agree with him, at least partly, but still not want to pin it down. I'd never even heard the word "theme" used in this way before our conversations. I've always simply jumped into books and lived in them.

"If you boil it down to a message, one message," I say to him one day, "then you make the whole thing into something too simple. You can just tuck it away, like a puzzle you've done, after you've finished. A book should be way more than that. It's a whole world! Or if I'm going to like it, it has to be." I want the place I go into when I read a book to be too rich and intricate for me to even want to reduce it to some theory about life. "If the writer wanted to say something so simple, why would he go to such trouble to invent all those characters and everything?"

"Oh, you're quite right," he said. "There is more to it, and an author doesn't necessarily know at all what his theme is, even as he is writing the book. He may see it at the end. Or one would hope he would. But he writes in obedience to some inner necessity — and something of his vision of the world informs what he writes. Wouldn't you agree? So you could say that that vision will at least implicitly carry a message, even if not consciously."

"I just want for there to be room for my imagination to move around in a book. I'd hate to feel I was just being told 'what's what' by a writer. I'd be totally bored."

"I agree that would be tiresome. A theme has to come across subtly or the reader will get restless. Being preached at is no fun, and a book before anything else has to be engaging — I'd say entertaining but that sounds too trivial, but that's a crucial element all the same." He talks sometimes as if I'm a whole class in front of him not just one girl, but that's okay with me. It makes me feel important, that he feels I'm worth explaining things to. I also sense that he is talking about himself with all this. His own books have messages. I sort of like that about them because I learn about Canada, but it can get in the way.

He talks a lot but he does ask me questions and he really listens to what I answer. "Is he a pacifist would you say, then?" We are on about Remarque again, and I sit beside him and I think and then I put my thought into words, all the while watching his face. "Did you really draw that conclusion?" he may say. "That's an interesting angle."

He seems perturbed by the fact that I don't have enough historical background for these European novels I'm reading now and he talks to me about the movements of history. He goes way back in time to the Greeks and the Romans. He tells me about his own studies. He was a Classical scholar. It's clear he thinks my education is being pretty paltry. He often tells me how unprepared his students always are because schools now are so slack and I assume he means it to apply to me too. But I think he doesn't realize that I probably know more than most people my age just because I do read so much. He's a professor at McGill University, as well as a writer, but I'm not sure how much he knows about young people. Of course, he has no children of his own. Anyway, he's definitely right about the bad education I got this past year at King's Hall. When I look back over it, it seems to me that most of the emphasis was on how to be a lady. That was all about "don'ts": don't eat in the street, don't call out of a window, don't ever turn around in the street no matter what is going on behind you. (That one sounded downright dangerous to me!) And trying to make us acquire English accents by chanting certain verses in assumed English voices while Miss Gillard went up and down the rows checking our vowels. Now I'm no longer there, I can think those things were funny. Miss Ramsay's math teaching was good though, I have to say that, and somehow the liver business didn't change the way she was with me in class. Though I didn't entirely trust her.

Something coincidental is that Mr. MacLennan's only sister teaches at the school. She didn't teach my class but I used to see her. I was interested that she was his sister, even though I hadn't yet talked to him and was just admiring from afar. She made me feel uncomfortable, sorry, the way I would feel about the unmarried maiden aunt in a novel, or for "the Daughters of the Late Colonel" in Katherine Mansfield's story that Carol and I were just reading. She never got to be an aunt, even, and she looked timid and walked in an almost stumbling, swaying, yet careful, way as if she were almost too frail to be moving along. Her nickname was Pussy Foot. She was very thin and grey-haired and yet her face was quite pretty if only there were some life in it. She gives me the same feeling Mother's cousin Mona does. Mona is so bossed by her mother, still, that she is like a person who has never grown up even though she is elderly. Mother has told us how, when she was a child, her mother never let her run, lest she fall. Imagine getting towards the end of your life and you have never, not even once, run over the earth, felt your legs move like that. It's pitiful, truly. Anyway, I don't know who could be bossing Miss MacLennan. It makes me wonder about the MacLennan family though. How did the daughter of the family get to be like that, while he got away and went to Oxford, and got to be a writer and so on? And to be vigorous — that's the big difference between them. It would be impossible to imagine Miss MacLennan on a tennis court. I don't use her nickname. It seems cruel to me. Most things about that school were cruel. I repudiate that sort of cruelty.

All this time I have been lying on the dock staring down into the dark green depths. It is too deep to see the bottom and sunrays beam up towards me in yellow ladders.

Mr. MacLennan is not coming. It's almost time for the noon whistle.

As I paddle back across the lake it occurs to me: the word is *constancy* not *constance*. I sing in rhythm with my strokes: "He who would valiant be 'gainst all disaster, let him in constancy

follow the Master . . ." I really like the spirit of the hymn.
Especially the verse that seems to express my King's Hall time:
being surrounded by those besetting me with dismal stories.
Fighting with giants – not very accurate, that; there was no one
worthy of being called a giant. But there were so many ranged
against me that they can count as one giant maybe. But the
point is, being ever unbroken. I was ever unbroken.

Bunyan wrote the hymn. A Puritan (I am not as ignorant
of history as Mr. MacLennan thinks). Then, many people had
names that were qualities. Men gave their baby boys righteous
names about striving and battling for good. Sometimes a name
could be several words even, something along the lines of Be
Righteous in Battle, or Always Endeavour, and no one would
dream of calling a baby boy one of them now. But the girls'
names have lasted, some of them anyway: Faith. Prudence.
Patience. Hope. Even Charity is a name, I think. It's interesting that they are all meek qualities. They all suggest being
quiet, being careful and good. Waiting. I prefer a more definite
and fierce role.

So what about the name "Anne"? I can't judge it, being
inside it. But I like its being a simple name, one sound. It's a
yellow name to me. Days of the week have colours too and
numbers do. I wonder if this is yet another thing that is peculiar about me or if lots of people see things like this.

In the afternoon I go over to my friend Patsy's house to
see if she wants to do anything. Her family is the only one at

the Club from the West, which is interesting, and she has two older brothers, which also interested me, because I wanted to see what it would be like to have older boys around, but they didn't pay any attention to us and now they're off at some tennis camp. Patsy and I were quite close friends last summer but something has changed and we now don't have as much in common as we did. Then, we were both still reading all the Arthur Ransomes and I had with her my first long talk with a girl my age about books. We were walking along River Street after supper and I can still recapture that thrilling feeling of things opening up. It was wonderful to discover someone else who knew all those people: the Swallows and Amazons – John and Susan and Titty and Roger, Nancy and Peggy.

For a long time, my sailing adventures and all my explorations were coloured by those books. From when I was about ten until just last year, I spent a lot of time imagining I was living in the north of England, the Lake District, with a lake longer than it is wide like Lake Massawippi, with a little village at each end (in the books there is a further village halfway along one shore). On the lake the children sail small boats that are exactly like my dinghy. The low wooded hills are like ours too. When we were first here in the winter, it was just like *Winter Holiday*, and Chuck and I explored everywhere in a way you can't possibly do in summer, climbing the hills through the leafless trees and when the snow came, going on snowshoes or our terrible skis. Or we would go way down the lake on the ice. Not that the children in the book had skis or snowshoes. They just had sledges, and they had skates, which they got to use more than we did because our ice was so seldom clear or smooth. But everything else was just the same. The book landscape was somehow realer than the real one. It affected how I saw everything, and imposed itself as if I'd entered a new visual language. And language itself came into it: we were climbing fells, sliding on frozen tarns, crossing becks. Patsy at least to some degree shared that world. Now I am living in a different one, mostly Russian. It's made a gap between us.

There's another thing too. Her father. It happened a few times last summer but I'd hoped he'd have forgotten about it; I'd more or less forgotten about it myself. I have an excellent memory for most things, but there are some things I just let slip away. Or that's not accurate: I sort of fuzz them out on purpose so I can't remember them. But now I am thinking of it because I'm hoping not to see him, that it will turn out that he's gone back to Montreal.

However, as their screen door clicks behind me and Patsy calls down that she'll be ready in a minute, I suddenly see him. He's at the far end of the verandah stretched out on a wicker chaise longue reading the *Gazette*. I'm in the sun and he's in the shade which is why I didn't see him at first. However, right away he's on his feet and coming along towards me. For such an enormous man he moves pretty smartly. He gets between me and the door so I can't back up and go out to wait on the steps. Maybe I'm sort of frozen too because I should be able to move faster and yet don't. He's my friend's father. He's a grown-up. It would be impolite.

What he does is always the same but just a bit worse each time. He says, "Well, Anne! You're getting to be such a big girl now!" He speaks in a falsely hearty voice, as if I'm a much younger girl than I am. "Let me see if I can guess your weight!" Then he grabs me to him, fast – I never seem able to jump aside properly – and pulls me right against him, against his stomach, and hoists me up in the air so I am dangling with my feet off the ground. I am quite a tall girl but he can do this because he is so large. My dad is six feet but this man towers over him. I feel like a doll, helpless, and he is squeezing me and puffing and almost giggling as if I'm a great weight he has to struggle with, which is absurd because I am quite thin. I am sort of squirming from side to side, trying to get down and also to keep my face away from his but I'm powerless in his great big arms. Finally he drops me. I know I am red in the face and my blouse is all untucked.

He leans down and puts his great pink hand on my thigh and squeezes, actually pinches, the way someone might pinch a chicken to see how fresh it is – I don't know why I have such an image. I've never bought or pinched a chicken myself.

Maybe it's because I feel like a thing, not a human. Or at that moment want to be. But he is smiling and still panting a bit. The whole stupid thing — which he's done before so it isn't even anything new — excites him as if something quite thrilling has happened between us.

We both hear Patsy clattering down the stairs and he gives me one more little smile as if we've shared a nice secret and goes back and picks up his paper.

I don't plan to tell anyone about this. I've never yet told anyone. Maybe sometime I'll tell my sister Carol. I couldn't possibly tell my parents. It's such a small thing, not worth making a fuss about, and yet it feels like more than that in its humiliation.

Patsy and I head down to our boathouse to go swimming. As we go, I feel what has just happened move to the back of my head. I shove it into a little cupboard there.

Later, on my way home for supper, I take it out, just a little way, not really looking at it, so I can think about it a bit, philosophically. Men puzzle me more than I can say. But I puzzle me too.

Two years ago when our house was being redone, I had a big crush on one of the painters. I used to help him, climbing up to work beside him or passing him what he needed when he was doing things up a ladder by himself. I learned a lot about how you go about painting a room. He was much younger than Patsy's father, but still of course an actual man, not a boy.

He was twenty-five, in fact. He had bright brown eyes, like caramels, and thick brown hair that was bleached a bit by the sun so that it was lots of colours. One day, I went into the house and he was the only one in there. He came along the hall towards me. The light was dark gold: late afternoon sun was pouring into the rooms and the walls downstairs hadn't been plastered so were just the colour of the wood and yet at the same time it was shadowy because of being in the hallway. Everything was quiet and yet sort of echoey because all the furniture had been moved out while the work went on. He looked at me, not smiling the way he usually did, but intently. He came right up to me. I just stood there. I had a feeling of something buzzing in the air. He put his arms right around me and he gave me a kiss. The kiss was amazing: I'd no idea until that moment that people used their tongues when they kissed, that the man's tongue went right into the woman's mouth — in my case, the little girl's. I can't say I enjoyed it; I was so totally surprised. But I didn't exactly not enjoy it.

I was only twelve and I had had this extraordinary thing happen! After he did it, he smiled at me. He always had a very sweet smile. And then he simply walked on and out of the house. It was the end of his working day. He picked up his lunch box as he went out the door.

Carol was still more or less at the same level as I was then. That is, she hadn't moved ahead as she has now into the Next Stage, so the first thing I had to do was find her and tell her.

That was when I learned that the tongue business was something that happened more generally. Carol had heard talk that suggested that was so. It wasn't just a funny and rather rude quirk of the painter's. We were both electrified at what had happened and that it had happened to me first when she is two and a half years older. Of course we never told anyone else.

He never did it again. I'm not sure if I wanted him to or not. I liked the idea of it more than the reality. In the experience of it, startling, exciting, a bit disgusting, it was nothing whatsoever like the thing with Patsy's father. In a way I rather wished he'd do it again just so I could pay more attention. I wanted to figure out more about it. And I still liked him. I know it was wrong, what he did, but even when you know something's wrong you can still find it exciting, and even hope for a bit more of it.

Mr. MacLennan. He is not at all like either Patsy's father or the painter. Not at all. Not at all! Is he Mr. Rochester or Prince André though? He's more Mr. Rochester, perhaps. Jane called Mr. Rochester her Master.

I arrive at the house and the family are just getting ready to eat. "Anne, my darling," my mother says, "I was wondering where you were." But she is smiling as she sets a bowl of new potatoes on the table and takes off her apron. She doesn't worry about what I might have been doing. I am allowed way more freedom than Carol is now, an advantage of being young and stalling in childhood as I partly am.

We are having roast lamb, which is my favourite meal, and I run and get some mint for the potatoes from outside the back door as that's my job, to gather the leaves and snip them up with the scissors. Rather a small job: I'm afraid I don't do much domestically.

I am now fourteen years and two weeks old.

I am sitting in the pasture with Mr. MacLennan. It's the first time I've encountered him here though I come up almost every day. It's not much of a pasture as far as animals go. Every summer since I was about ten, I've considered it my territory (no one ever comes here except Carol and Chuck and me, and I'm the main one who comes) but there have always been only two cows, Daisy and Dolly, and sometimes one horse, sometimes two. They belong to Grant LeBaron. When I was younger, Chuck and I used to go along after supper every day and help him milk the cows. He'd just tie them to the rail fence and sit on a little stool he brought. He has grey hair but a young, handsome face and he talks in the Eastern Townships voice I like; he makes two syllables of cow, for example, kay-ow. His daughter Mary became a friend of mine when I went to the North Hatley school. The pasture is actually owned by a grumpy and mysterious old man called Joe Sampson. The mystery is because he's somehow connected to our family, another of those shadowy things. In this case I have a feeling it's something criminal, not something that Old Joe did, but closer to us than that. It could just be that if he's a connection, even just by marriage (I think it's his wife who's the one), my dad doesn't care to acknowledge someone who looks as he does, never properly shaving or tucking in his shirt. But that doesn't really fit because my dad isn't a snob in other situations.

The pasture slopes upward, is dotted with old apple trees and groves of maples and clumps of wild roses, and has the cows' paths criss-crossing it. At the top, the land suddenly gets much steeper and there is a dense forest of mostly maple trees. Beyond the forest, the land levels out again and there are a lot of wild raspberry bushes. I know every inch of it.

We are sitting about two-thirds of the way up to the forest and the land falls away below us, so that we are looking over ripe grasses that are full of flowers — buttercups and daisies and devil's paintbrush and pink clover. Buttercups and clover blossoms are the flowers that please me most for some reason. They're not necessarily my favourite flowers but even the thought of them makes me feel contented and somehow safe. It must go back to something when I was really small that I can't remember. They seem the most innocent of things that grow, to me.

We are sitting there looking out at the hillside all laid out before us. Beyond the sloping meadow there is a row of bushy trees, behind which are cottages but the trees hide them, and then there is the lake. From here it is like dark blue silk.

Beyond the lake, running all the way to the horizon, there is a patchwork of little light green fields and darker green woods over which cloud shadows are moving.

I am perfectly happy at this moment.

"I think it is possibly the loveliest view in the world," Mr. MacLennan says. I turn and look at him, at his profile, and then at his whole self. He is lying back on his elbows. His shirt is rolled up quite far so I can see his tanned arms which have some light brown curly hair on them. The shirt itself is light blue and old: I can see that the collar, which is open, is worn and frayed on the inside, with little threads sticking up. His legs are crossed and he is wearing old jeans. I think of his legs, how strong and muscular they are under the faded blue cloth. I can even smell him, cigarettes, and soap, and also a bit of man-smell, of sweat, but a good smell. He turns his head and smiles at me. He knows I was watching him.

I wonder why he is here, if he saw me from his car as I climbed the fence. I have an idea that he did and that he came on purpose even though he pretended to be surprised when we met on the path.

"You know Harry, at the Club," he said. "You were watch-ing me play tennis with him yesterday. He was in a prison camp in the war, for three years. A Japanese one. They were appalling. Many people did not survive." I do know about them, in fact all too much, from an article I read in *Time* mag-azine when I was only nine. I had waking nightmares for ages from the descriptions of the men cooped in tiny cages too small to stand up in, crouched in their own excrement. "What saved him was this view, right from here. He used to come here as a boy, the way you do now. In the camp, he could close his eyes and imagine himself back here. Otherwise he would have gone insane, he told me. Completely insane. Or willed himself to die."

He turns on his stomach and lays his head on his arms and closes his own eyes but goes on talking, though it's a bit muffled against his arm. "It makes you wonder. How some people survived that. Even with this to remember. Could a person make it work?" His face has a closed, sad look. I'd like to know why he hadn't been in the war himself but realize it might be too personal a question. He often laughs when I ask a question no one else would dream of asking, according to him, but this is not the kind of question to make anyone laugh. If he wasn't brave enough, or healthy enough (though he seems healthy) to go, it would be a difficult thing to admit.

"I know about that sort of imagining, to keep sane," I say. "I know it's not nearly as ghastly, but I used to do that at school, when I finally would be alone, in bed at night."

He opens his eyes and is ordinary again and smiles. Not that he thinks it's funny at all, as he says, "I don't like to think of you unhappy."

"Oh, I can stand anything," I say. "That's the good thing about it. I know I've been my unhappiest and nothing can be as bad again, and I did it. I did it! Got through, I mean. When I was allowed home — every three weeks we were allowed home for Sunday dinner, if we lived near enough — I would stand at a particular spot along the lake road where the bank is really steep down to sharp rocks, and I'd want really badly to have the nerve to hurl myself down. I thought if I had a broken leg, I'd have to stay home."

"You might have done something far worse than break your leg, Anne. You must never consider anything so destructive again."

"I think underneath I was too sensible. That's what held me back really, probably. It's hard to know about yourself, though, isn't it? What is really at the bottom of what you do — or what you don't? You know in *Jane Eyre*, how she almost perishes, after she runs away from Mr. Rochester. Well, I think she was right to run away. But I think she was not a girl to let herself almost die like that. But maybe that's because I think of her as me, when I read that book. And I think I'd always end up doing what I had to, to survive — I would have run away, I think, but I'd never have been out on the moor like that, with no food and everything. I would not have lost my purse, for one thing."

Even as I say this though, I wonder if I really would have run away. I feel differently now because of Mr. MacLennan. I picture Mrs. MacLennan caged on the top floor of his cottage: no, I have to imagine a larger house. Say she were caged in the

Yellow House. But, crazed and sometimes yelling? We'd have to silence her somehow. But would I be able to resist staying, having him, even with Mrs. MacLennan raging around in a remote wing? Now that I am experiencing love myself, I see how it might complicate things. I might not have been able to make Jane's strong choice.

"But it's good to have suffered the worst," I say. "King's Hall will be the worst for me, for my whole life. I know it."

He stares down into the grass, then picks a stalk of timothy to chew the end of. "That's the value of those sorts of tests that life offers," he says. "It gives you the power of mastering stoicism. If you can survive something really rigorous, it gives you power to take on the next thing."

"Yes," I say. "And you can use good memories as ways to lead yourself out of the moment – like Harry in the prison camp. It really helped me that I'd been noticing, really noticing, what is beautiful all my life, or as far back as I can remember anyway. And I have all those memories there, like pictures, to call up in my head." But that makes it sound too easy. "It only works for me when I'm alone, though. When people are being vicious, right at that moment, I can't do it."

"Can you remember the first time you did that consciously, noticed beauty and knew you were noticing it?" he asks.

"Well, I can," I say. "I was six, and I was sitting on the old wooden fence between our house and the neighbours'." I love this memory and yet it makes me sad too. "My head was all among the lilacs, the flowers and the leaves, and I could see them in every tiny detail and smell them. They were that very dark purple kind, and I could see some of the little blossoms that had fallen down into the rhubarb leaves below, that had already turned brown. It was those fallen blossoms that made me so conscious. Because they meant time was passing. I knew that the very second I was in — well, that it was perfect. And that it was already passing, even while I sat there."

"There's sadness at the heart of beauty."

"Yes, there is! But it makes it more beautiful somehow, doesn't it?"

"Yes. We are 'in time.' We cannot stop it. We cannot step outside it. It's what makes life so precious, and yet it is remorselessly moving us along."

"Oh, I don't want to leap past my life! I wish I could slow it down. Don't you wish that? At some moments of course, not at the bad ones. I'd like to leap over those. But I remember on my ninth birthday realizing how fast it might go." I pause, seeing that early morning in my mind's eye.

"Tell me about it," he says.

"Well, I was sitting on my grandmother's bed and she was giving me her present, and I was just about to open it. It's funny, I can't remember now what was in the package, but I can still see, perfectly, the wrapping: it was white with little silver stars and tied with a pale blue ribbon. And the card had a bluebird and a yellow rose. It was a perfect moment. Being about to open a present, and Grandma always chose good things, but it was also to do with being there alone with her, as if there were something important about that. And then Grandma suddenly said: 'I can remember exactly my own ninth birthday and it feels as if it were today. It feels as if I am exactly the same person, and still nine.' And she smiled at me. She wasn't feeling sad herself. She wasn't feeling sorry for herself for being old now. But I felt — I hardly know how to tell what I felt!"

I rather wish I hadn't started this; it sounds too fancy and complicated and yet I want to understand it. And probably it's something perfectly simple that everybody feels. He is watching me attentively. He is very patient when I am trying to understand something, even as I talk, which is one of the nicest things about him.

"It's very confusing to describe and yet I know I'll always remember that moment. It was maybe as if Grandma and I were the same person. No, that's not it — more, as if somehow we were expressions of the same thing. And at the same time, it's as if we were both on an escalator and she was just farther up but for a moment, she somehow joined me. Which made me feel like crying."

Even as I tell him this, I feel tears rush into my eyes and I hope he doesn't notice.

"And yet there she was, so old. She was way farther up on the escalator! And it was moving — relentlessly! Yes. And fast.

And it made it seem as if my life could be over in a flash. She was once nine! And now she was so old! Oh dear." I have to laugh at myself. "It was just about death really, wasn't it? I guess it's really perfectly simple. It's just what we've already said. About time. You said we are 'in time' and we cannot step aside. My escalator – that's kind of a babyish image – but it's the same thing. It's just the fact that we will die and the people we love will die. It does make life almost too precious to bear, sometimes. And most of the time we don't even think of it, or I don't."

"Yes," he said. "I think that's what it is. And it's only at rare moments that we can truly look it in the face. You had one of those moments. Most of the time we pretend to ourselves that death simply cannot happen, not to us, not to the people we love. And then some little thing – that is really of course a big thing – shocks us into awareness of it. Or it can flood over a person in the middle of the night. That can be a hard time to keep up the pretense."

"Oh, I know about the middle of the night." I have always had trouble sleeping, or staying asleep. And that's when worries can crowd in, or did when I was away at school. Even at home there can be a lonely, really desolate feeling in the middle of the night, when I feel the horrors of the world that I can't even guess the extremity of – the things people can do to each other, as in the War – that can never be really vanquished, and are waiting out there. And other nameless things.

I want to hear something private from him. "Tell me something from when you were young," I say. "How did you become able to bear things yourself?"

"Well." He pauses and I wait. "When I was a boy, I used to sleep outdoors," he says. "It was a sort of test though at the same time I liked it. I liked being out in the air and the sense of nothing between me and the stars except a tent – or often not even that. But it gets pretty cold in Halifax!"

"Do you mean you slept out even in the winter?" I am intrigued by this and right away wonder if I can do it too.

"Well, yes. That was the stoic part of it."

I am lying quite close to him, our legs are almost touching. But we never actually touch. I think of him as a boy, as my age, fourteen, lying outside under the winter stars. Perhaps awake and staring up. Perhaps sometimes fearing death. I wish I'd known that boy, but of course he existed long before I was born, has long since turned into the man who is stretched out beside me.

"There would be ice all along the rim of my sleeping bag, from my frozen breath. I wore a tuque of course, as most heat is lost from the top of the head. It was rather crazy, in all likelihood. But what I would do was – well, I learned that if I didn't move at all – no shifting and turning, even when I was asleep – I could maintain just enough heat in the bag that I didn't utterly perish."

I am impressed. "How long did you keep it up? Did you do it for years?"

"Oh, forever! That is, until I went to Oxford. So – until I was fully a man."

I suddenly thought of his poor sister, her meekness, the way her body seemed ready to crumple at any moment from sheer ladylike gentleness and fragility. Where had she been while he had been doing this training and testing of himself? Had she, like Cousin Mona, whom she reminded me of, been told never to run, never to exert herself, so that all her muscles turned to tapioca, and running would be out of the question even had she tried? Her poor thin blood would never have allowed her to withstand sleeping out of doors. Or so I imagine.

My mind hops back to Harry and prisons. There is something I'd like to tell Mr. MacLennan.

"I can tell you something quite amazing about a sort of prison," I say. "It's very strange and you may not believe me but it's true. It's about a Mrs. Rochester person, the first one, I mean, who was up in the attic, hidden and crazy. There's someone like that in the village." I don't want at this point to tell him that there are in fact two, as that would make it altogether too unlikely to be believed. The thing about Club people, and he is one, even though he's a lot else as well, is that they have a very simple understanding of North Hatley. They only see a fraction of what goes on here.

"Is that so?" he says.

I want him to believe me, but chances are, he won't. It's too odd a story. In fact it's just like a story. That's the problem. I sit up straight to feel more important, to add credibility to what I am going to say.

"I was with my friend Christine. Christine knew about her already, this mad woman. If she really was a mad woman. I actually got a little idea that she might be a relation of Christine's."

I consider telling him about Christine but decide to leave it. Christine is someone right outside any world a Club person could recognize as a human world. When I was at the North Hatley school, I soon understood that of the poorer people there, there was more than one general kind. There were, for example, the ones who came from sad-looking rundown farms, farmhouses that had never been painted and whose walls were the same grey, splintery wood as an old dock. The whole place would be all overgrown, and usually there would be a few old wrecked cars and parts of an old truck and tractor and bits of other ancient rusty machines lying around in the yard. If I was ever inside one of these houses, I never got beyond the kitchen which was where life happened, and it was always absolutely full of bits of things, mostly broken things, just smaller ones than those outdoors. These were heaped in about-to-fall-down piles on every surface of counter or table and on top of the fridge, if they had one. When they had a meal, they just shoved back some of this, enough to put down a plate. All of the stuff around made the room dark, though the windowpanes that were sort of misted with dust contributed too.

One girl in my class came from an extreme version of a place like that (I was in it once) and she arrived at school every day in the same faded dress that was really a woman's and draggled down to her ankles. But she and her whole family were accepted as perfectly okay. On the other hand, a few families who were not necessarily even as poor as that girl's were absolutely not okay. The Stinkies were that sort of family. Of course that wasn't their real name but they were all called it: the dad was the original Stinky and there were all the little Stinkies. Christine was the oldest of these and she was in my class and twelve too. I liked her. She also wore terrible dresses but she had a look I liked. Her skin was very pale and she was quite tall, with pale brown, straight hair cut straight across just below her ears, I'm sure just done by her mother and in a hurry too. But there was something fierce and proud about her as if no matter how scorned she was, she'd just stare back at the scorners. They lived in a shack just up the hill, quite close to the village but not in it. Her dad was tall, fat, and bald and her mother was skinny. You wouldn't have necessarily known it to look at her, but her mother was very young for that husband and for all those children. Christine told me that her mother had been married when she was only thirteen and had Christine when she had just turned fourteen. It occurs to me that maybe that's why the village was so mean to that family and called them the Stinkies: Christine's father "interfered" (my mother's word for what is done to a young girl by a lecherous man) with her mother and got her pregnant. It seems extremely unfair to blame the whole family but that's the way things go. And that they are poor is a big part of it, if not the whole of it: someone like Patsy's father "interferes" like mad and gets away with it. The Stinkies have moved away now; one day they just weren't there any more. The shack was empty. I hope wherever they've gone, they've escaped from the name and that it doesn't catch up with them.

Mr. MacLennan would be unlikely to have ever known anyone of the Stinky type.

"Well?" he says.

"Christine was a friend of mine at the North Hatley school," I say. "She was pretty different from me — her family was very poor — but I liked her and we used to do things together sometimes. We never went into each other's houses but sometimes I'd look out my window and she'd be sort of almost hiding behind our big maple tree — she never dared knock at the door. Anyway, this one time, there she was, and I knew she was hoping I'd come out. So I did, and she said she had something to show me.

"It was after supper, and it was one of those first spring days when the evenings were already getting so that we could play outside for a while and it would still be fairly light. Christine stood there looking sort of excited. 'I want you to come with me and see something,' she said. 'Or really it's that you'll hear it. You won't see it.' So we headed down to the village.

"Once we got to the village, she made us go right around by the little lane behind the barbershop. We were right down behind the Hob Nob Restaurant. Then she made us scramble into some bushes where we had to crouch over and crawl along almost on our hands and knees."

Mr. MacLennan is watching me. He's smiling a little bit. But even though it was quite a while ago, I can still feel the urgency and furtiveness of that scrambling. It's not a funny story to me.

"It was all shadowy under there and I got mixed up about exactly where we were, and then suddenly she was saying, 'Shh,' in her fiercest whisper and I saw that we had emerged more or less — she still made us try to keep hidden — right near the trestle bridge and in sight of Bonneville's Store.

"In front of us was that little hut, someone's tool shed it looks like, no window and really small. You must have seen it." I look up at him for agreement. But typically for a grown-up, he obviously has never noticed the little shed. "Well, anyway, it's there, in full view of the bridge. There was a padlock on the door. There still is. So, Christine pulled me right up close to her and said, just hissed really, 'Listen! We may hear her!' This was quite spooky and it was odd that it was, because we were so close to everything and yet she was being so intense. And she was scared herself. I could tell she was.

"And then we did hear something: it was crying, very, very quiet and sort of hopeless crying, almost impossible to hear, and yet just barely, barely, we could hear it. Maybe it was more a whimpering. It was the saddest sound.

"And then we ran. As soon as we were back on the road, I kept asking her, 'Who was it?' We were standing in front of the Hob Nob now, both of us breathing hard. I said to her, 'Who is *in* there?' But she wouldn't tell me. That was what made me think it was maybe some relative of hers – either the prisoner or the jailer, or both. She was scared the way you are when you know the person and the danger.

"Inside the Hob Nob, people were sitting at the counter eating hot dogs. We could see them through the windows. There they were, and it seemed amazing that the ordinary world was just going on as usual and we'd just been close to something so horrific. Could we really have been? Really? Seeing those ordinary people – Doreen, my mother's cleaning woman, was one of them, and her boyfriend – everybody in a row, sitting there, laughing and eating. It made it seem impossible that a woman could be trapped in that little shack so nearby. I already started not to quite believe it. But I know it's true really." I stare at Mr. MacLennan, daring him not to believe me. His face is skeptical.

I have to finish the story – or as much as I know. "That

was the last time I saw Christine, which is maybe some sort of clue – but of what? Her whole family disappeared right after that night. But I think the woman is still in there! Actually, I'm sure she is. The padlock is still in place, but sometimes I can tell that someone has been in and out – her keeper, it must be – as the grass is squashed. He must go there only at night. I told my sisters about this because I thought someone else should know but they thought I was making it up, 'as usual' Ruth said. She never believes anything I say." I regret the last point: it sounds so young.

I can tell Mr. MacLennan doesn't believe me either. He knows I don't lie, but he thinks I was taken in by a trick, that I am mistaken. I'm not. "No one could be cooped up right there, Anne," he says. "Someone would be bound to hear her – someone other than you two little girls. I really think that girl – Christine – was playing a trick. She was teasing you. And it was probably starting to get dark, wasn't it?" I nod, unwillingly, because that had nothing to do with it. "She worked on your imagination."

However, I know she is there, that woman.

Maybe it's the same old thing: men have to be allowed to do what they need to do, even to the point of jailing a wife. I assume she is a wife. No one really wants to say anything. Other men, nice ones, men like Mr. MacLennan or my dad, would never do such a thing themselves, but they would think it was none of their business — if they ever believed it in the first place. For instance, lots of people must have known about Mrs. Rochester and no one did anything. That was a long time ago and only in a book, but it was modelled on real life. And things in villages haven't changed so much, that is, the hidden things in villages. In any case, that woman behind the Hob Nob is not the only one in our village. Someone like Mr. MacLennan is too innocent to know about such things. Which is a funny thing to think, when he is so much older. But I don't bother to tell him any more about mad women. I don't want to spoil our time by getting him to think I'm crazy or obsessed by something ridiculous.

He takes out a cigarette and fits it into his holder. I like his hands. Actually they are very similar to my dad's, who has the nicest hands I know. Mr. MacLennan using a cigarette holder — I think it may be ivory — is somehow fine with me, even though we have a thing in our family that holders are affected, especially for men.

We are quiet for a while, both sitting up now and gazing out over the view. The cloud shadows race across the distant fields. A few sailboats tack across the blue water, so tiny I can't even guess whose they are. I rest my chin on my knees. "Anne," he says, "I don't doubt that you believe there is a woman in the shed."

"And I'm right, too," I say, because I cannot resist. I turn my head and I smile at him. He looks at me for a long moment. I stare back. There's something very full of meaning in the way he looks at me, and I wish I could read what he is thinking but of course I can't.

I can almost see Mr. MacLennan's hand reach out and circle my ankle. Only it doesn't. He does not bridge the couple of inches between us. But there is an almost fierce feeling of restraint in the air, a sort of active restraint, of energy held back. It's as if we are both holding our breath.

He sighs then and so do I. I guess we were, in fact, both holding our breath.

"We'd better get back," he says, and gets to his feet. He doesn't reach out a hand to pull me up, either; not that I need help getting up of course, but it's the kind of thing my dad would do automatically, just for friendliness, if he got up first.

We walk together down the pasture and he branches off to climb the fence and go along his road, and I continue down through the thick clumps of milkweed at the bottom of the pasture. I pick one of the pods and peel it open. I've done this every summer; I like the crinkled white silk that is inside.

It's Tennis Week. I've been watching the men's singles. As the week has progressed, it has got more and more tense. There really are only two contenders for the championship: it will be either Mr. MacLennan or John Bassett. I like Mr. Bassett. He lives across the road from us in a big white cottage that they rent from the Wileys, and his three sons, Johnnie, Dougie, and David have been friends of my brother's and mine forever. They are close together in age, all of them between Chuck's age and mine. Mr. Bassett is very large and very noisy in an invigorating way. Whenever he bursts onto a scene, everything livens up. He's handsome, with gold-blond hair and very bright blue eyes under bushy eyebrows that bleach out in the sun, and a big, jutting nose that gets red and peels. It might seem more likely for me to be in love with him rather than Mr. MacLennan, because he's more dramatically good-looking, but for one thing I've known him too long and always heard all his conversations, or feel as if I have because his voice is so loud, and there's also being a friend of his boys and of his nice wife. But even more, it's that feeling of suspense about my relationship with Mr. MacLennan. He intrigues me; there are shadows in him.

I try to analyze what I mean by those shadows and why I like them: they give me something of what I feel when I'm reading. He's like a person in a book, though that's combined with the fact that he writes books himself: he seems to have all the dimensions inside himself of other worlds and people, or I can imagine he does. When I read Tolstoy, I'm in nineteenth-century Russia, completely – I live there – and I see it as night-black, shot with colour and lights. On every hand there are interiors or landscapes that are like dark tapestries, those scenes of winter nights and people flashing along on sleighs under fur rugs through the snowy emptiness, and then the darkness of battle smoke, and suffering, and the sadness of the Rostoffs on the move across Russia, exiled from their home. There were sunny scenes of course, the scenes of Kitty and Levin in hot summer fields, in *Anna Karenina*, or cozy scenes, like when Natasha is finally safe, married to Pierre and triumphant over her baby having a healthy bowel movement, rushing to show the others the diaper. But the whole thing is more alive because danger, awful risks, and death are everywhere just below the surface or have just been survived. The contrasts make everything so much sharper. In the Brontë novels, there's darkness too and more steadily. Even when Charlotte or Emily describes a scene of sunlight and birdsong, it is impossible to believe in it or see it in your mind because you know the darkness has merely retreated momentarily. It will soon be back. There is a movie of *Wuthering Heights* that I've never managed to see (and it has Laurence Olivier and so I long to) and I hope if I ever do see it that it proves to be in black and white, as colour would not do at all for that book.

Mr. MacLennan is not Russian and I'm virtually sure that he has never lived in a mysterious Yorkshire house where maniacal laughter echoes at night, but all the same, still he is a figure of shadows, to me. I think he's not a happy person really. I'm not sure exactly why I think that but it's a feeling I have.

To watch the matches, we sit above the courts where there is a very dense row of pine trees. There's a bench in the shade of them but that is claimed by adults, and kids sit or lie on the grass. Everyone comes as the week draws to an end and it's the men's singles that are by far the most exciting. The reason it is so gripping goes well beyond tennis. For several years the same two players have been in the finals. Both are terrifically proud, and winning is a huge thing. They are closely matched and one year one may win and the next, the other. Mr. Bassett is a few years younger and I know Mr. MacLennan is extremely intent on besting his rival, who in other circumstances is a friend. Of course he makes out in the lead-up that it doesn't really matter. It's all for the fun of the game. But it's clear from the way they go at it that this is far from the truth. As they play matches that are closer to the finals, they both get redder and redder. Sweat streams off them. You really hope one of them doesn't drop down dead. It doesn't help that Tennis Week, as usual, is the hottest week of the summer. In the past, there have been some terrible scenes after the winner has triumphed. There is no pretense then that it doesn't matter: the loser has been known to hurl himself onto the grass and almost smash his racket with the strength of his beating it against the ground, in sheer rage and temper at having been defeated. They appear to feel no shame about these displays and everyone is thrilled by them of course. But woe betide the day when Mr. MacLennan loses two years in a row and Mr. Bassett is established as the best for good. At some point this is going to happen, a final defeat before the swift racket and swift legs of Mr. Bassett, or of someone even younger. There are other good players coming up.

This year, now that he is my particular friend, I am hoping strongly that he succeeds. I don't want his pride injured.

I lie watching and am aware of his wife sitting not that far away, on the middle of the bench. I prefer to ignore that she even exists, and as far as our friendship goes, she doesn't.

Their marriage is a total mystery to me. She is not at all pretty and she is bossy, like a headmistress, though more so than any actual headmistress I've encountered yet. She is large, not just tall, but with heavy arms and legs and a strangely low, large bosom. She is considerably taller than he is, I think, though funnily enough I can't be sure how much taller, maybe because now I can hardly see her for the dislike and discomfort I feel when she's there. Her hair is grey and she has several – perhaps three – chins. Her voice is low and plummy. I only hear it when she calls him from inside their cottage sometimes, if she sees him talking to me when I pass their garden, or sometimes at the Club she'll peer out of the gloom where she is having her tea indoors, and call him away from me. He doesn't always go, either.

They don't seem like any other married pair I know. They don't match. He is so lovely and she is so very much not. She really is ugly. It might as well be admitted. I am cruel about her but I can't help it. She is very unwell, too, or that's the story. Like someone in olden times, she had an illness as a girl that has weakened her for good. Even that doesn't make me kind, I'm afraid. I just feel sorry for him being saddled with her, instead of being with a healthy, young – girl. Aye, there's the rub, as Hamlet would say. I am just a girl, a mere girl. When we are alone together, we seem so close and then when other people are around I see the nonsense of my imagining any sort of – any sort of what, exactly? I don't even know. I had such improbable daydreams before, and the more I actually get to know him, the more confused I am.

I shove away the thought of his wife. I watch him racing across the red-brick dust of the court and swinging his strong brown arm, sending the ball smoothly over the net to just where Mr. Bassett fails to be in time to smack it back.

Mr. MacLennan wins. The two men come almost staggering off the court and he stands bouncing his racket against his knee and grinning. Both men are scarlet and breathing fast and their hair is dark with sweat. Mr. Bassett laughs in his huge bray, throwing back his head and baring his particularly large and white teeth. He aims a pretend-fierce punch at Mr. MacLennan's shoulder, which is in fact quite powerful and makes him step backward. It's really a pretend pretend-fierce punch. However, whatever chagrin he may feel he trounces swiftly, more swiftly I'm sure than Mr. MacLennan would have succeeded in doing had the win been the other way around.

I am pleased for him but I walk away and head down to the Club where I've left my canoe. I don't like it when there is a bunch of adults around that he has to pay attention to, and especially that his wife is one of them.

On my way up the hill from the boathouse, I come across Mr. Buckland digging a ditch; there must be trouble with the pipes at someone's cottage. This is quite a common occurrence as all the pipes in the village are ancient and tree roots intertwine and break them. He is a friend of mine and I stop to exchange a few words. I like his voice which is like Grant LeBaron's only more so, and I like his comfortable way of leaning on his shovel and plucking at his cap, his way of greeting me and showing he's ready for a chat. He's quite an old man to be working so hard but he loves to dig. He has often said to me, "I've just always liked digging; it's the one thing I like to do," and he plans to go on as long as he can. I often meet him walking through the village on his way to or from jobs and he is quite distinctive. He walks with a bend at the waist, leaning forward, his shovel over his shoulder, and he's never in any sort of hurry. He wears his trousers high up towards his armpits, hitched there by braces. When I was younger, I used to help him dig but now we just talk a bit – about nothing much. Ruth has said to me, "what can you possibly mean that Old Buck is a friend of yours? What can you possibly find to talk about?" It's not something I can explain. I like it that the village contains such different versions of being a person. My dad is the same as I am in this; he has all sorts of improbable friends.

When I was at the North Hatley school before I turned thirteen and went to boarding school, there were boys in my class who were maybe going to be Mr. Bucklands when they got to his age. They even wore their pants the same way, including the braces, and they sat at the back of the room. They seemed men but they couldn't have been sixteen yet because as soon as they reached that age, they could leave for the mines. I gathered that they had been sitting around at the back of Grade Seven for several years, but they were no trouble to any of the rest of us and just waited out their time, and patiently as far as I could tell. Our teacher, Miss Stark, didn't appear to be a cross woman but somehow no one dared kick up in her class.

Times I loved at that school were the late afternoons in the winter when the lights would be on and the classroom windows would be gradually turning a darker blue as the snowy light failed outside, and Miss Stark, would let us draw while she read to us from *Silas Marner*. And I knew that soon I'd be outside and running down the slippery hill to see if I could hitch a ride around the lake on one of the big horse-drawn sleighs that pulled logs. The kids from up the Minton Road went home by a sleigh that went across the lake ice. It was like a box, that sleigh, with no windows and a little stove inside.

※

Grandma and Auntie are leaving today having had their three weeks. I'll be sorry to see them go. Aunt Hazel seems a calm and contented person and yet her life has been so much smaller in scope than her younger sister's, our mother's, that it could be seen as sad, looking at it from the outside anyway. She's not at all the sort of meek soul that Miss MacLennan or Mother's Cousin Mona is: she plays golf and she skis, and she's a much more in-control teacher than Miss MacLennan manages to be (I was in her classroom for a day once), but her life has been almost completely one of service to my grandmother. I am interested in the different ways women's lives turn out because I often wonder about my own, what path it will take. I won't be content to be a spinster. Definitely not. I want someone dramatic to marry though. I am excited by power and danger in a man.

In my mother's family there were very definite roles, and very strong favouritism that was quite open. There was an older sister called Catherine, who died when she was thirteen. While Catherine was still alive, Aunt Hazel told me, their father insisted that she always sit by him at the dinner table. She was so beautiful he liked to look at her and rest his hand on hers while he ate. Hazel was in the role of the plain one and sat down the table out of sight. This strikes me as the cruelest thing and yet she tells it as if it were quite under-standable. Their father, my grandfather, was a minister (like all the men in that family, on both sides. We have pictures of rows of ministers in their white surplices, all brothers, or cousins, or brothers-in-law) so you might think he'd be more sensitive, but apparently he wasn't. In a different conversation, Aunt Hazel told me that she had only two foods she could bear to eat as a little girl, pork chops and corn. She doesn't seem to notice that there might be a connection between these two things — hating almost every kind of food and being banished away from her father's sight during meals. After Catherine died, my mother, who is five years younger than Aunt Hazel, became the Beautiful Daughter — and she truly was beautiful. The dead Catherine, despite her father's adoration of her, in the one picture I have seen of her, was not as beautiful as our mother. And Hazel, even if less lovely than her sisters, was not plain. But somehow her role was to be that. Both the sons died; Edward, the oldest of all, in the First World War, and Ellis, the youngest, before he even got to his first birthday, so then there were just the two girls. Mother got to marry a handsome man who took her off across the world to all sorts of new experiences and to be a mother of four children, and Aunt Hazel got to stay home forever. Pretty unfair.

My father's childhood was sad, in ways he won't speak of, but he rose above it and became a brave venturer in the world, and if I were a man he would be a good example for me to follow, but the things he did would still be hard for a woman, likely impossible. As soon as he graduated from McGill, my dad went out to Africa to look for gold. Instead he found copper. Later, in Canada, he found gold.

In our den we have various artifacts that are just in a jumble on the shelf and we often take them down and play with them and he doesn't care. He doesn't see them as specially precious, but each one holds a whole story, which my dad will tell if we ask. The stories about Africa feel like the background of my own life, even though my parents came back before I was even born. As with the Lake District and Arthur Ransome, and now with Tolstoy and Russia, it's another whole imaginary world that is often more real than North Hatley.

There are two jambocks, which are terrible things, or were meant to be. My dad never used them because he hates any physical cruelty, but they are long whips thicker than a man's thumb, and they are curled back on themselves in a sort of hoop. They were meant to be soaked in water so that they would unfurl, and then they were used to beat "boys" with. "Boys" were African men. One of my father's colleagues beat a "boy" so hard with a jambock that he badly broke his own hand and lost a finger when it got really infected. That was a lucky stroke of justice, in my view, and in my dad's too, though the man is still somehow a friend.

There are little stoppered vials that contain clear liquid in which floats a needle threaded with catgut. They were meant for self-doctoring out on the bush-veldt, when a man was torn or chewed or clawed and had to sew himself up. Sometimes I hold one of these in my hand and I imagine the circumstances, a lion's teeth, for example, having ripped my leg, and how bold I would have to be to plunge the needle in and start sewing. I hope I would have the nerve and I guess I'd jolly well have to. No sewing machine to thread anyway.

There are two chunks, the points, of elephant tusks from an elephant my father shot one day, urged on by his "boys" who wanted the excitement and the meat. One of them had to run for miles to get a permit after the shooting, while the animal was already being carved up into lumps by natives who appeared out of the forest with baskets. The gun had only been a 303, which was actually too low a calibre, but he was a good shot and it had worked.

The men slept in tents and often at night would hear a lion roaring. "It's the most terrifying sound in the world. It booms and reverberates through you, right to your heart and to the marrow of your bones."

There are pictures on the walls of the den of those "boys," standing in twos and threes, carrying spears. Their teeth are filed to points and some are tattooed in the old way, which my dad has described: "They cut themselves in patterns, and then they rub dirt in, and the cuts fester, and when they heal, there are raised scars and that's the tattoo." Their feet were tough as leather. "One of them stood accidentally in the sleeping coals of the fire, and no one, including him, realized what the burning smell was for some time."

Once, an American attached himself to my father and was desperate to shoot a lion, something my dad didn't agree with as they wouldn't eat it, but the man did it anyway. Then he did the second mistaken thing, despite my dad telling him not to: he followed the lion, which he'd only managed to wound, into the long grass. My dad knew the lion would wait for him and savage him, and that is just what happened. So my dad had to shoot the lion himself and then, with the "boys," carry the stupid fellow the hundred miles to the hospital. It took four days. Every night when they stopped to rest, the stink was worse as the gangrene spread. He died just as they arrived at the hospital. "Never follow a wounded lion into the long grass." My father always ends the story with this warning.

I love hearing these stories, even the grimmest ones, probably especially them, but they make me wish I were a man and so were able to do such adventurous things out in the world.

It's a wild day. The wind is whipping down the lake and the waves are huge. The sky is dark and ominous: a storm is brewing but it will take all day to blow itself into real rain and thunder and flashing lightning. Meantime, the wind. North Hatley is a great place for summer storms. I love watching them race over the countryside and down the lake and I like to be out in them.

I am planning to take my boat out. No one else is on the lake which is a situation I enjoy, being the only person ready to risk it.

Just as I arrive at the boathouse, Mr. MacLennan's car comes along. He stops when he sees me, of course. "My God, Anne, you surely aren't going out in that?" He waves his arm out the car window at the wild water. What with all the sounds — the trees are seething back and forth and the waves are leaping and dragging at the stones on the beach below — I can hardly hear him. I go up close so I don't have to yell, grabbing my long hair back as it starts to blow into his face. I know I must look as wild as the weather but the wind makes me bold.

"But it's the best kind of day! Come too! Come with me!"

Usually he is the one to suggest anything, but this time I do. I wonder if he is as brave as I am, as brave about being out on the lake in a storm.

I know that he's not someone who can let a dare pass.

It will be interesting to see if I glimpse white knuckles.

My dad's friend Dr. Frohberg was here earlier in the summer and I took them both out. It was a windy day then, too, though not as bad as today. I could soon see that Dr. Frohberg was terrified. I don't like to think I'm cruel, but maybe I am a bit because there was something satisfying about a man being frightened and my being completely in charge. My dad knew it was okay of course. He was a Sea Scout on Lake St. Louis when he was a boy and nothing can scare him about wind and small boats.

I rig the boat with some difficulty as it is leaping up and down and I don't want it to get bashed against the dock, but finally I am ready. Mr. MacLennan has been sitting on the dock, steadying the boat as best he can with his feet and getting quite splashed. "Should we have life jackets?" he asks at one point. But Chuck and I are always scornful of life jackets and we don't have any good ones anyway, just some little-kid ones that my younger cousins use when they want to swim out as far as we do. They'd never go round a man's chest.

We are both fairly wet by the time we set out. Once we pull the painter in and push off, we are free to accept the force of the wind and not fight it any more, and we are instantly racing out and across. The water is dark and wild with whitecaps breaking all around us and tossing spray which flies in our faces.

I tack across as close to the wind as possible for the maximum speed and the maximum heeling over of the boat. The water is whirling by almost at the level of the gunwales, but I know how to keep it just that little bit below. I've no intention of shipping serious amounts of water. We tack back and forth, moving gradually farther and farther up the lake, past Yellow House Point, past Hovey Manor. Soon we are well beyond the buoys used as markers for the Club races. The lake is much wider here, maybe two miles across, and it is like in *We Didn't Mean to Go to Sea*: we are racing into the unknown – we will continue on and on. We will arrive sometime – tomorrow, the next day – in France. Or Holland.

I am loving it.

Now I turn and I look at Mr. MacLennan. I want him to be loving it too. Mostly. At the same time a separate part of me has been showing off and relishing my power, and wants him to be scared, as I am not.

He isn't loving it.

His hands, his square, capable, tennis-playing hands, are tightly clamped to the gunwale and his fingers are white with the intensity of his grip.

It suddenly occurs to me: what if he can't swim? I don't dare ask; it would be too embarrassing, a grown man unable to swim. He must be able to. But he has no waterfront, no boathouse, and I've never seen him in the lake. Oh dear. And his face is grim.

I widen my eyes wildly at him and grin, hoping he'll smile back. And he does. But, "My God, Anne," he shouts – he has to shout it is so noisy. "My God, Anne, what are we doing out here? We must be crazy."

"It's perfectly okay," I yell back. "Really. Really! But –" I swing the tiller across – "watch the BOOM!" He gets his head down in the nick of time. "We'll start back."

The wind is now behind us and I pull up the centreboard and let the sail out completely. "This is the loveliest part," I say. "Running before the wind. Just relax. Relax!"

I am the one in the reassuring role for once. It feels very satisfactory and grown-up. We fly along extremely fast but it is now smooth. We slide, we glide over the water – really it feels just like flying – and the boat is level, not heeling over which I guess is what bothered him so much.

We sit close together in the stern now and he has unclenched his hands and shoved them up inside his sleeves for warmth. "I've never been used to very small boats," he says. "That's what makes it so alarming. On top of which, we seem to be the only people rash enough to be out here." He has to be cross because we both know he was scared for a bit there. But I don't mind. His hair is all wet and plastered against his head.

Coming up against the dock means another bad moment for him. Chuck and David and I have figured out a way of heading straight for it and then, at the last second, turning into the wind, so as to come gently on alongside, usually. Nothing can be exactly gentle today though, with the strength of the wind. "Grab!" I yell at him as we are about to slide right by, and he manages to catch the top of the ladder at the end of the dock.

I take down the sail and he helps me drag the boat up the beach far enough to be beyond the waves. It's not the sort of day when I can leave it tied to the ring on the dock. We then both stand on the boathouse verandah and I get us towels from inside as we really are sopping. He rubs his hair and it stands up in short, wild curls. His old corduroy trousers are dripping wet and I can tell his running shoes must be squelching. I never wear shoes myself when I go sailing.

But he is laughing now, not furious as I was afraid he might be. It's a bit of a fake laugh but he's doing his best and it gets more real. I guess he feels glad to be alive, since he seemed to think there was some question about it.

He looks unbelievably handsome. I wish I dared hug him, but I don't. Of course I don't.

"You really are a wretch, Anne. You knew it was out of the question out there."

"But it wasn't!" I say. "Here we are, safe and well!"

"Come on. I'll drive you up the hill."

As we run up the steps to the road, the rain simply plunges down on us in a sudden, solid sheet of water but we can't be any wetter than we are, and we tumble into his car, bringing a lot of the rain and lake water in with us. We are both laughing now; for a little bit I feel almost as if we are the same age.

The summer is coming to an end. Arrangements have been made for me: I am going to go to Havergal, in Toronto, and will be boarding for the first few months until the family move there, at which point I can be a day girl. Somehow I am not worried about the boarding part. For one thing, it won't be for a whole year, but also I have an optimistic feeling about it. From what I've seen in the brochure and heard about the school, it sounds completely different from King's Hall. It's much larger; it's quite beautiful. One of the distressing things about King's Hall was how ugly and down-at-heel it was. It even smelled bad. The Havergal teachers, in the descriptions of them, sound like real teachers, not just sad and bitter old ladies who are trapped there. I am prepared to hope for the best.

But I don't want to leave North Hatley and, specifically, I don't want to leave Mr. MacLennan. Next summer feels a very long time away.

On my next to last day, it is raining again. Fall is around the corner and there are even yellow leaves here and there among the dark green and on some trees whole branches have turned. There have now been several quite chilly nights and the lake is already colder.

I am walking along the road by the lake and hardly anyone is around. No cars pass me and I realize that quite a few people have already returned to the city and the cottages will soon be boarded up. Our family will return from Toronto for Christmas though, my sisters coming from McGill (Ruth) and Bishop's (Carol). But I can't think of Christmas and I just feel gloomy.

I likely won't see him before I go. On a rainy day like this, he may just stay indoors. I picture him sitting writing, or reading by the fire — everyone lights a fire these late summer days. I likely won't see him. I collect our mail from the Post Office and tuck it inside my rain jacket. Nothing for me, needless to say. A couple of years ago I had six English pen-friends I got from *Collins Magazine*, which is an English magazine I still get because I like the atmosphere: everyone who writes in is an Arthur Ransome fan, and the stories are in that vein, so very much my type — or the type I was — and I used to enter the competitions and win prizes of books, novels by Noel Streatfield, or anthologies. And letters to and from England, and Scotland too, whizzed back and forth. But somehow the pen-friendships have dwindled away through my not being able to write from King's Hall, being too miserable. My thoughts circle over my past, interests I've abandoned, friends lost. My gloom deepens as I head back through the village.

Then my spirits leap: he is coming out of Bonneville's with his *Gazette* and he waits for me.

"I have to take a book to someone up on the Sherbrooke highway," he says as I come up to him. "Why don't you come along for the ride?"

Because I am being with him for the last time this summer, I am especially conscious of every bit of him. I study his wrists and his hands, those hands that clenched on the gunwale so hard when I was scaring him on purpose. That was just a week ago and feels like longer. We still had a week to go, then. I want to memorize each detail so I can call him up when I am lying in my boarding-school bed after lights-out, and this idea then makes me horribly lonely in advance; I'm still with him and already I am swept by the bleakness that I'll feel when I'm hundreds of miles away from him. We usually have a lot to say when we drive along like this but today neither of us seems able to talk. The only sounds are the wipers and the wet hiss of the tires on the black road.

Suddenly I say, and I can't imagine where it comes from, as it just emerges from my mouth of its own volition somehow, "I sometimes wish you were my father." It's a lie and I never lie to him but I can't unsay it.

I see his grip tighten. We are going slowly up the hill past the Pleasant View Hotel, out of the village, and the rain is falling harder so that the windows are getting a bit steamy. I am totally confused as soon as the words are out of my mouth.

It's not true and I don't know why I said it and, as well, I feel real consternation on behalf of my own dad that I've said something that seems to wipe him out. And I feel further horrible dismay at I don't know just what. I am embarrassed, is part of it. I don't wish he were my father at all. It was a truly stupid thing to say.

But the car is pulling over and stopping. He draws up under a huge, dripping maple tree. There are a few yellow wet leaves plastered on the road in front of us. I stare at them and then glance sideways.

He looks straight ahead and closes his eyes. He takes a big breath. "That's the nicest thing anyone ever said to me," he says. The car is full of emotion as if the air has become thick and heavy. But it is full of distress too, I don't know whether mine or his. I realize I had wanted – no, it is stronger than that. I really needed – to say something to him to express that I feel something huge for him. But I don't know how to say what it really is and so it has come out all wrong. It has put me into a child role that feels as if it cancels out all our talks and walks, and the afternoon in the boat, and I've done it myself.

I don't say anything more and sit there quietly but my heart is jumping. I frantically want to know (oh I badly, badly want to know) what he feels, what he thinks. I know that inside his head, he is as real to himself as I am real to me. But the mystery of another person baffles me. And he is a man, and so much older. I push my hands into my pockets and clench them into fists.

He doesn't speak.

The thing I have said has made everything so strange.

He is almost always the one in control, the one I try to please and amuse and astonish with my brilliance. I like to make him smile; I like to impress him. I know he likes me and all summer he has minded if a day or two went by and we didn't see each other. He'd say, "Where have you been? I looked for you."

He is a grown-up! I don't know what goes on inside a grown-up.

With the wipers turned off, the windscreen is a blur of water. Maybe only a couple of minutes have gone by but it feels like a long time. And still we sit in silence. I can smell the mixture of smells that I will always associate with him, accentuated by the dampness.

He still has his eyes closed.

He has a whole life that goes on when he is not with me. Which is such an obvious fact but somehow I never manage to take it in. I think of him only in terms of me, as if he only exists when I come on the scene.

I am too old for such a silly way of seeing the world. I am being now the way little kids are when they can't imagine that their teachers have lives and go home to husbands or boyfriends.

Maybe I am just a tiny part of his life. I will leave North Hatley and not see him until next summer and he won't mind a bit and will forget all about that we became friends this summer. Or whatever it is that has happened.

I stare again at the blurred yellow leaves.

I am about ready to scream if he doesn't say something soon, and especially if he doesn't open his eyes soon.

I have said something that is not true. Or maybe there is a bit of truth in it. I do think he would be a good father for a person to have. But I don't want him for my father. I just want him, though I don't know what I mean by that exactly.

Now at last he opens his eyes and he is looking at me. He smiles but I can't make out what sort of smile it is. There is something different in it. "Oh, Anne," he says. "Oh, my dear Anne." And that's all he says. He sits still for a further moment and then he starts the car.

A SWIM

There is a memory that I cannot place, nor can I extend it. It hovers tantalizingly as a fragment. Was it still the summer I was fourteen, or might I have been fifteen? I don't think I was as old as sixteen because there is something still of the slipping back and forth between seeing myself as a child, or wanting to, and the acceptance of being almost grown-up.

It is a fragment that has the quality of a dream and yet I know it is not a dream. Only in memories of my very first years do I confuse the two.

It is extremely hot, tropically so, and steamy with it. The air is so full of moisture that one's clothes cling damply as soon as one puts them on. It is a day to spend entirely in the lake, though the lake itself is almost as warm as blood.

I am swimming in a direction I don't usually go, west of our boathouse, and I am slowly breaststroking along parallel to the shore and near in, very near in, so I can swim under the willow trees that hang low over the water. I have never swum under here before and it is like jungle-swimming, as if I am up the Amazon, with thick leaves and branches like fronds over-head and sometimes trailing over my face. I am within a green light, which is what gives the dream feeling, as well as does the warmth of the water and the slowness with which I move my arms through it.

And then – he is there. Mr. MacLennan is there.

Amazingly and at the same time completely naturally, because this is almost a dream, or a movie we are in, he is in the water, where I have never seen him, and he is right there, close, his face quite still with surprise, and younger with it. The intense heat must have brought him down to swim at someone's dock and he too has drifted into this green cave-place. I assume he has come from the other direction or I would have seen him. It is pure chance. He is in an inner tube – that is, he has it under his arms; he is not lying across it – so I still do not discover if he can actually swim.

We draw even closer together and I tread water and then realize I can almost stand, which I do, on my toes, with the lake up to my neck. He is wearing a bathing suit of course, or perhaps it is an old pair of ordinary shorts, but it is the barest he has ever been with me, and we are in this other element, water, which makes everything possible.

It makes touching possible. For the very first time I reach out my hands and put them on his body. I put my hands on his shoulders.

I slide them down and grip his upper arms. I want to wrestle with him, the way I wrestle sometimes with my friend David, either in the water or on the living-room floor. This part of the memory makes me think I must have been only fourteen still. Would I have seen wrestling as the route to intimacy if I'd been any older?

I try to duck him and of course he won't let me – and how can I, anyway, when in fact we both can touch the bottom, even if barely. There is no sense in what I am doing. But we do, in fact, wrestle – for how long I don't know. And how exactly does he fend me off? Where are his hands? What has happened to the inner tube? It is maddening not to remember but the crucial tactile images are lost.

And then he turns away from me. I remember that. I still have my hands on him. He is within the circle of my arms and my hands are on his stomach, lightly, no longer fighting him. I may even rest my face against the back of his neck. I think I do.

And does he turn around again? I don't know. My mind will not release anything more.

Many years later, a friend tells me a story: she is swimming in the sea off Cortes Island. It is early evening and the tide has come in over the rippled white sand, which is warm from the heat of the day's sun. She is swimming naked, as everyone does off Cortes Island, and the water is pale green with the sun still shining through it, and she can see the tiny weeds like dark stars, below her on the pale sand. She knows it is the most beautiful place in the world, and that the most beautiful thing she has ever done is this abandoning of herself to the gentle movement of the water.

A man swims up to her. She has seen him before but only from a distance and has never spoken to him. He is naked too. He looks like a gypsy except for his heavily lidded eyes which are a clear light blue. Without a word, they embrace. They make love in the sea – and it is love; they are tender and they laugh in delight though they do not speak – and then he smoothes back her wet hair, kisses her forehead, and they swim away from each other. She never sees him again.

I tell my friend's story because I see how one tale echoes the other. Both are mythic: there are the mermen lovers, and there are the women who are free of ordinary land morality.

In the innocent element of the water, they can abandon themselves. They can touch, embrace, and be themselves touched and embraced. And swim away. Nothing has really happened. Only a brief encounter with a god.

But my story ends quite differently, and I am sure of that even though I cannot remember. At fourteen or even fifteen I could not have slid my hands down Mr. MacLennan's stomach and into his shorts. And if I had been the sort of young girl who could have done that – well, perhaps I could have seduced him. But then he would not have continued to love me. Or so I think.

So why do I include something so very outside the realm of what we could have done? What has my friend's erotic moment off Cortes Island to do with this story? My needing to slip it in here puzzled me until I saw that my older self, and not so much older, could easily have behaved as my friend did, and part of me wishes I could somehow tinker with the truth. Could I not – as if I were positioning puppets – move my later sexual experience back in time to allow me to seduce him? After all, I am recreating this, and who would know if I cheated? But, no. I cannot do that. I could not have behaved like that as a young girl, any more than Mr. MacLennan could have behaved like the gypsy man.

But I will not seriously twist truth. I want my account to be as clear a reflection of who we actually were as I can make it. That is where the interest lies for me, for me and I hope for you, in our constraints, in the tension of what didn't happen, as much as what did.

So I leave in this odd scene to show you how I am not cheating. Though I could have.

xo

So, everything I have told here is true. It is true to my memory of those long-ago emotions. Of course I may have mixed up times – for example, did Mr. MacLennan really win the Men's Tennis Singles in 1950? I certainly watched him win, but was it that year? No doubt it is on record somewhere at the Club, or John Bassett's only surviving son, Douglas, might remember – though he likely wouldn't. He would not have had my degree of interest in that match.

The woman hidden in the shed is real though I have moved her back in time. I will tell more of her.

I have simplified. My life was full of other things that summer too, that first summer of my friendship with Mr. MacLennan, the summer which was to set the course of how things would be one summer after the next, until I was eighteen when something changed it, at least a little.

My sisters in this account are shadowy figures and I have not described how we sang together while we did the dishes every night, new songs like "Some Enchanted Evening," or "On a Slow Boat to China," and also the ones we had always sung, "Green Grow the Rushes Oh!" and the old English rounds. Or how Carol and I still had many conversations about books, about Club people, or about her ventures into being grown-up, tales which I found alarming but often funny, too. There was a lot of laughing in our house. And music: not just our singing, but the piano, Mother's Beethoven Sonatas, and the Chopin Mazurkas and Waltzes I played constantly that summer, especially the ones in a minor key which expressed what I could not say.

Despite all that, much of the time I experienced the isolation I have described. No one knew the extent of my relationship with Mr. MacLennan. Looking back, I realize I was almost incredibly free to fill my days as I wanted to and I was very self-contained, a combination of the usual early adolescent absorption in oneself, and also my having a different kind of time than my sisters had had at my age.

I was eccentric – even if not to the degree I thought I was. In talking about that time with Carol now, I discover that she felt rebuffed by me a lot of the time, that I appeared to occupy a secret world and gave the impression that I thought I was superior for doing so. That may have been true to the extent that lonely children often will imagine themselves to be superior, as a defence against suspecting they are peculiar in some way. I also have largely left out my brother and yet we were still close, still sharing our child-world of swimming and boats. He was probably the one who knew most about the amount of time I spent with Mr. MacLennan, but he would never have told on me, or indeed thought there was anything worrying to tell. And our friend David Pollock, closer in age to me than Chuck but friend to us both, was an almost constant presence in our kitchen and part of everything Chuck and I did.

But my intent is to explore my relationship with Mr. MacLennan. I have focused on it to the exclusion of almost everything else because it puzzles me so, even more now, far more than it did then. And it got more puzzling as it went along – as it did go along, for seven years. I have to wonder in what way and to what degree it played a part in the mistaken and destructive choice I was to make.

And there is something further: I think I may have betrayed him.

But that comes later.

ENTER A DARK STRANGER

*T*hrough three years at school in Toronto – my new school, Havergal, which suited me as King's Hall had not – and through my long holidays in North Hatley, I moved up time's escalator, in my old childish image.

I left Havergal after Grade Twelve, just before I turned seventeen, ready for the adventure of living in Montreal. I could enter McGill University without Grade Thirteen, which would have been required had I stayed in Ontario for university. Ontario seemed dull to me always, compared to Quebec.

Patterns meantime had been set. In part, I had set them myself, willing my life to be as I wanted it. I sought to keep myself strong and independent, and I was those things at least for my school years. While I liked the school and the other girls, I did not develop very close friendships. As far as I could tell, most other people, girls anyway, lost their young true selves as they got older. I wanted badly to stay what I felt to be my real self, the person I'd first recognized as distinct and clear-edged and bold when I was about twelve. I wasn't sure if it was possible; it was worth fighting hard for though. I also had long since given my heart to something that had powers far beyond what I realized. Literature, my great joy, was shaping my imagination and would determine my choices. The natural world was still forming me too. My communion was still more with trees and water than with any human being of my own age. That I isolated myself gave books even more of a chance to shape my dreams. Being alone with nature fed my strength; literature created models of women who were at the mercy of their own passions. And my apartness was going to mean that those who loved me were not going to dare to try to influence me. I did not see the significance of any of this. I assumed my choices were entirely in my power and could keep me free.

Not being at a public high school meant I could bypass all the fraught trials my sisters had undergone to do with clothes, makeup, boys. I wore my school tunic during term, and in North Hatley, my old uniform of jeans or shorts. I had an old army shirt given to me by one of the visiting African friends of my dad's. (I always fell briefly in love with these men.) It had been worn on the North African front and was battle-torn. Grandma mended it for me and I wore it till it fell into shreds. But disavowing feminine trappings was not going to be enough. My breathing the air of the early 1950s meant I was daily taking in that which was going to sap my strength. I listened to the radio as I did my math homework and all the songs said one thing. I went to movies with my friends; I read magazines. I heard other girls talk. Everything and everyone said the same one thing — love, love, love. Love is all that matters — and it didn't seem important enough to defend against. These things happen so softly.

The heroes of my daydreams stayed the same — fictional ones. And Mr. MacLennan. When I was not in North Hatley, Mr. MacLennan — and I don't know even now if this is odd — was hardly more real than the others. I needed his physical presence, actual or at least imminent, to believe in our friendship. It never entered my head to write to him. I suppose I still considered he could not possibly think of me if I weren't before his eyes.

I am back in North Hatley but it is already August, a later arrival than I've ever had. It is dismaying to have missed all of June and July, but I have had my first summer job away from home, having completed my first year at McGill University. The job was not for very long, only six weeks, and I enjoyed it — I looked after two little boys on an island in Georgian Bay — but to have lost almost a season here hurts me. And now I feel a dislocation: the trees are into their older-summer selves, their leaves hang heavy and dark, and the pasture is full of goldenrod and milkweed, the earlier summer flowers over. And yet I have not had spring, not real spring which for me must be here in this place, in order to count. I have even missed strawberries. But at least am in time for raspberries.

I hope Mr. MacLennan is in town. I want to see him and wonder, my first morning, if I'll walk by his house. Then I decide not to. Best to leave it to chance. Tennis Week is over, another excitement that went on without me, and I worry that he may have headed off to Nova Scotia, where he often goes for a visit at some point in the late summer.

There is also the man I met briefly back in June, before I went away. There was something about the look of him, and his voice. He even entered a dream I had, afterwards, though I had only talked to him once. I wonder if I've exaggerated my dramatic image in the weeks since. I'll soon see.

It takes me a full day to realize I am actually here. I am restless and unsettled, and taking it out on my poor mother who is washing my clothes, and I still haven't seen Mr. MacLennan, though I've been to the village twice. I do catch a glimpse of his car: he has not gone away yet. Good. I wonder if he has wondered where I've been.

In the late afternoon, I walk to the village again, this time to talk to Emily LeBaron. I am hoping she may hire me to help her in her antique shop, the Flying Shuttle. I've spent a lot of time, over the years, helping Emily, not for a wage but just because I like her and she shows me how to do things. We have stripped furniture together, exacting and hazardous work involving lye, and sometimes, in the Easter holidays or at Christmas, I've spent hours at her side, both of us painting the cards she makes — line drawings of village scenes with little capering figures skating, or leaping into the lake, according to season, or dancing around the bandstand at a concert — and we colour them in bold childish colours. Once we even took an evening art class together in Sherbrooke, going over on the bus as she never has had a car. And we've gone for walks together, late fall or winter rambles, when we go way up over the hill above the pasture, often ending up dropping by the house of one of her friends, Mrs. Cate or Mrs. Virgin, who will give us tea.

Emily is important to me for various reasons and one of them is because she is a version of being a woman that intrigues me. Could I ever be like her? For several years I have been reflecting on what being a woman means; that is, what it will mean for me, as I can't help relating everything about this subject to myself. I still worry. I will with all my powerful will that I not ever be confined, and yet some trap may lie in store for me, attempt to avoid it as I might. I vow I'll not tumble into some dull domestic swamp. But what if I don't recognize the quicksand until my feet are deeply mired and I cannot drag them out?

I study the women I know and consider the ways in which I would want to be what they are, or, in most cases, would not want to be. I want to be a mother just like my mother, but I want to be more. There is a lot about Emily that I admire and would not mind being.

But what about babies? Emily has had no babies and I know I want them. Two would be safest. That way, if I needed to flee, I could clutch one under each arm and run for it. I can see myself clearly, racing across a wide field, one baby astride my hip, the other, younger, clasped firmly around its stomach and face down. What a strange thing to picture. It seems to assume that the swamp is inevitable. For a while. Maybe a person has to enter it and hope to extricate herself. Otherwise – I don't know what. I want two things that can't go together.

In a certain way, then, Emily and I are close friends. In terms of the time we spend together it would seem we must be, but we are reserved, or perhaps it is just I who am, and who shies away from the personal. I would love to really talk to her; I sense she would be valuable to talk to, because she is older. I think she must be my mother's age, and it is odd perhaps that she is my friend, not my mother's. But the things I would really like to ask her or confide in her somehow don't get asked. What does she think of my relationship with Mr. MacLennan, for instance? She knows more about it than other people because she has seen us together a few times in earlier summers, not that she would ever dream of spying but just because she walks in the same places we do. But she never mentions these encounters. I suspect she is waiting for me to do so. And I wish I could.

I go up her path and she is there on her verandah, sitting on the edge of it with her legs comfortably wide apart; her skirt is long and full, soft old blue cotton, so this is not unseemly. Her feet in her interesting shoes are squarely planted on the ground. These shoes are specific, in my experience anyway, to her and to Mr. and Mrs. Virgin, who get them in New York for the three of them. Mrs. Virgin is a New York millionaire, also a North Hatley cow farmer of extremely special Jersey cows, and a financial partner in the antiques shop. She and Emily have been best friends since they were girls. The shoes are rumoured to cost a fortune and are handmade for each person, looking like nothing so much as little square pieces of luggage, being of soft leather, folded and stitched. No other woman in the village would dream of wearing anything so eccentric but I would dearly love a pair.

Emily has never married but there is no sense in which the label of spinster fits her, as no one could possibly see her as "unchosen" or in any way pathetic or humble. She is as different a version of an unmarried woman from Cousin Mona, Miss MacLennan, or even Aunt Hazel, as there could possibly be. I feel quite certain that anything that has happened to Emily has been deliberately or even wilfully chosen by her. She could have married had she wanted to; she just must not have wanted to. For one thing, she is quite beautiful. I didn't at first realize this because she doesn't conform to any fashion or usual notion of feminine attractiveness. When I first got to be friends with her, back when I was twelve, I thought she looked like a witch — but a beautiful witch. Her complexion is quite dark though also ruddy and her eyes are large and black, with heavy lids. Even though her face is smooth and young, her hair is grey and falls to her shoulders where it turns up at the bottom all the way round. When she smiles her face comes even more alive and deep dimples appear in her cheeks.

She beams that smile at me: "Anne! Hello! You are back! Come and sit beside me and tell me everything."

I sit down and at once come out with my request: "I will, I will tell you everything," — which of course I wish I could, but know I won't — "but first you tell me something: will you hire me for the month of August to be your slave? I'll do cards, I'll serve in the shop, I'll clean the place, I'll strip things, I'll do whatever you command me to — what do you say?"

"Sounds good to me. I want a slave this summer. I've just been wishing I had a slave." And so we settle it.

"Someone has been asking about you," she says, looking at me sidelong.

"Oh, who?" I ask, feeling myself go pink with my sureness of who it must be, and also with my slight anxiety that I am wrong.

And I'm right. "Hugh," she says. "It was Hugh. He's been by a couple of times just wondering if I knew when you were coming back." She looks a little mischievous. "I told him I had no idea. I said I thought you weren't coming at all this summer. He looked quite crestfallen."

"You didn't!"

"No. I'm teasing. I told him I thought you'd be back at the end of the month of July. And here you are." This is the nearest we have ever come to the subject of what in the world goes on between Mr. MacLennan and me. It is an opening. But I can't seem to take it.

"When shall I start?"

"Whenever you like, as soon as you can."

"Tomorrow?" I want something to do.

"Sure. And we will be businesslike with this: be here at nine o'clock."

I had my birthday while I was away and am eighteen now. I loved my first year at McGill University, where for the first time I was one of a small group of people who were my intellectual peers: this was a revelation and I loved it. They were girls who had also lived in literary worlds, almost to the degree I have, one of whom listened to music as obsessively as I do, another of whom walked with me along Sherbrooke Street to our life-drawing classes (where the female model was naked but the male was allowed his dignity and a bathing suit), both of us imagining we were art students in Paris in some earlier era.

The girls are Canadian, American, and English; one is from Barbados, one from Bermuda, and all of us are new to Montreal. Right from the start, we spent considerable time, and all our allowances, drinking cups of tea or coffee, sometimes eating snacks too, sitting in little cafés – the streets that run down from Sherbrooke Street below the University are lined with them – watching the European immigrants with whom the city is flooded. They have been washed up in Montreal in the aftermath of the war and the closing of the Iron Curtain, through which they presumably managed to wriggle at the last possible moment. We were thrilled to have entered at least the fringes of an exotic world, a Bohemia filled with polyglot dark strangers. (Or sometimes fair. The Baltic men were fair.) We knew they must come from myriad fascinatingly fraught backgrounds about which we were prepared to be soothing and understanding and, what would be even more effective, impressed.

Most of us felt until meeting each other that we were more intense than other people. Now we were affirmed by one another and we could be socially bold. We sallied forth from Royal Victoria College, our hall of residence, to explore the new world we had arrived in. We walked everywhere in the city, at any time of the day or night, alone or in twos or threes.

If there was danger in the city, it did not come near us. I know we must have seemed schoolgirls still and that in our cardigans and wool skirts and our childish knee socks, we were a far cry from women of the world, and that likely went some way towards keeping us safe.

Nothing much happened to any of us, in terms of romance. No one found a serious man. But we dramatized our small adventures and laughed at each other's tales. I was intrigued by a young Parisian: I went out with him twice, enough for me to fall deeply for his green eyes and his French brush cut, which looked like fur, but I was too inexperienced for him and the romance went nowhere. His name, enchanting to me, was Claude. The other girls were content to accept dates with Canadian boys, but I required something more dramatic: I had been reading Dostoevsky and Arthur Koestler. I yearned for someone who carried the whiff of danger, and had darkness and suffering troubling his brow.

However, university has been over since early May and now that I am back in North Hatley, Montreal seems even farther away than when I was working at my summer job in Ontario. This is the home I love best. It's somehow a timeless place, and I am, within a day, submerged in it as if it is the only place that has ever existed. Which means Mr. MacLennan is now very present in my thoughts. The little wire of excitement that thrums in me when he is near is alive again. I won't look for him, though. He can find me.

After my first morning with Emily, I walk through the village by myself. I agreed to do just mornings, but long ones, working until one o'clock, and so I am starving. Tomorrow I must remember to bring along some fruit or some cheese to eat at eleven.

As I cross the bridge, his car drives up. I was somehow certain this would happen and don't even look around until he speaks to me. And then I just get in.

I am so glad to see him. I smile at him.

"I'm glad you're home, Anne."

"Oh, yes, me too."

I am still in love with Mr. MacLennan.

And so we start into another summer of being friends like this, secret friends. All these years, and it feels a very long time from my having been fourteen to my now being eighteen, he has inhabited his own separate channel in my life. I see no end to our relationship nor any way of changing it: I will always feel this way about him and we will spend time together and I will never quite be sure what he is thinking. That is how it feels, at least it has until now.

Something has changed this summer: we drive together, we talk, we sit on the Club verandah if no one else is about: all this is the same. But he watches me more. He studies me. Also, even though I am now older and not the child I was when this began, he is bossier. Or bossy in a different way, as he has almost always taken the lead. He needs me to knuckle under. I must take the university courses he tells me to and, more important, I must share his view of the world's descent into chaos. He is fearful of the social and political changes looming and he claims loudly that the old order is threatened. I listen to all this but I am free of these fears myself. I see the world and my future in it as exciting and challenging.

We sit in his car one day, the windows rolled down, both of us looking out at the lake, which is a serene blue, too calm for sailing. I think of that day I took him out and of how simple our relationship was, when I, however briefly, seemed his equal, even his superior, in terms of bravery and control. There is no question of equality at the moment.

"There are cycles in history, Anne, and it is important that you know this" – and I do know it; he has told me before – "There are patrist periods and there are matrist ones." The first time he talked of this, and it was last summer, for several minutes into the conversation I thought he was saying "mattress," and was utterly bewildered. "We are approaching a matrist one. The signs are there for those who will see them."

I find this theory of his tiresome but I have to hear him out. There is no stopping him once he is under way with a topic dear to his heart.

"A matrist period is terribly destructive of all that upholds the structure of our culture and our institutions . . ." I stop listening.

There is another reason for a change in our relationship.

That man I met who is the new Club Manager/tennis teacher.

I recognized him the instant I saw him, that one time at the very beginning of the summer just before I went off to my job, when I was in North Hatley for two brief days. He came walking down the Club dock just as I was beaching my canoe. It was a sunny day and there were white clouds racing across the sky behind his head. The lake was choppy with a light wind, very bright blue, no whitecaps.

He had dark hair, almost black, falling thickly across his forehead, and dark eyes, narrow and set slightly aslant. He was lean and tanned, clearly athletic, and that day was wearing a maroon sweater over a white T-shirt and white shorts, and below him as I was, on the beach, I was very aware of his strong brown legs. He squatted down to speak to me, his hands on his knees, and at once I liked his hands. "Good morning." I heard his European accent.

Then I had that dream about him while I was away. In it, he was in our house and he was there as a member of the family. It was a strange dream, given I had scarcely met him, but it had that power a dream sometimes can, when I know it is a warning. It was full of resonating emotion, a depth charge both thrilling and frightening. His black eyes stared at me; he was in our living room, an alien presence there but inevitable. It seemed then to me that even in that fleeting encounter before I left for Ontario, I had "recognized" him.

Thus my days run along two paths which are completely separate and do not cross over. I see Mr. MacLennan often in the afternoons, but in the mornings when I work at Emily's, I look up to see a dark young man stride up her walk – he is on his break – and he comes in to where I am sitting painting, or he waits while I talk to a customer. And then he pulls me into her sitting room, or into her kitchen, wherever she is not, and he puts his hands on me.

He was what I had wanted and I willed him into existence with my powerful will, to be the manifestation of the brood-ing hero I have dreamed over in my Russian novels, and in D.H. Lawrence and Thomas Hardy too. "Be careful what you wish for." I remember someone – Mother or Helen, my nanny, – saying that long ago.

And we also go into the Clubhouse at night (we are not supposed to be there, but he has the key) and sometimes, if it is cold, he makes a fire and we sit huddled before it and he tells me about his life. It is the very tale of Eastern European woes and imprisonments and flights that I have longed to hear. He threads his fingers through mine as he talks.

He tells me:

The Grand Hotel Toplice (which, he instructs me, is pronounced *Toplitza*). This was the scene of his childhood and boyhood. "The village of Bled is the most beautiful village in the world," he says and his voice has an elegiac tone, for he will never see his village again; that is understood. "It has everything that North Hatley does but each thing is more beautiful: there are not these mere hills you have; in the distance there are snow-topped mountains, the Julien Alps, and the lake is a mountain lake so that the water is very dark green, very deep." He stares into the fire as he speaks, as if he sees there the place that he describes. "Swimming in that lake is more wonderful. And there is an island you can swim out to, a tiny one, and there is a white church on it, very, very ancient. On the far side of the lake from the hotel – you can see it – is a high cliff and on it is a castle that was built there by the Bishops of Blixen." I can see it all too, and also that it is Eden, the lost garden, and that nothing can ever make up to him for his banishment from it.

"My mother built the hotel," he goes on. "That is, she designed it. She was as good as an architect, and then she ran it. Bled was the summer court for all the years we had kings in Yugoslavia and every spring, the King and his household and all the embassies would arrive and set up their establishments. Our Grand Hotel was for all the people who came from across Europe to be part of that."

His English is very good. Like his manners, it's a bit formal. Only the "th" sound is hard for him. In the middle of a word, it becomes more "s." And my name is "N." His manners I like, the way he stands very straight when he is introduced to someone and bows a little. Never clicking his heels though. That would be German and out of the question. (He hates anything German.) Before he lights a cigarette, there is a small half-circle gesture he makes with his hand, at the same time slightly tipping his head to one side, and he says, "*avec permission?*" I like these little things.

He shows me pictures and I study them in the light of the single candle. There is an old brochure of the Grand Hotel which I open out, and I see the huge marble swimming pool, which is surrounded by tall round pillars. Chandeliers hang from the high ceiling and shine down onto the water. He says, "It was fed by hot springs." And then, in another picture is the front of the hotel, all vine-draped balconies facing the lake, which is right there, directly below. And then we have the dining room — and people. There are tables around which are grouped what seem to me to be impossibly sophisticated Europeans, all dressed up in their 1930s summer finery, white linen jackets on the men, floral frocks on the women. They are smiling at each other as if oblivious of the camera and also, and far more horribly, oblivious of what is ahead of them: war and destruction and death.

As well as the actual photographs, the brochure itself, as artifact, its brown and white images and its slight tatteredness — it is torn in places along the folds from having been opened

and looked at so many times, and then refolded and put carefully away – speaks to me of what has been lost: a world.
Eastern Europe before the war. It existed, that perfect summer
Grand Hotel, back on the far-distant side of the pit of suffering into which they will fall, and soon, these people smiling at
their dinner companions, and also the ones waving and grinning from the lake in another picture.

"The Gestapo used Toplice as their headquarters for the
northern part of Yugoslavia."

He tells me:

He lived in that earlier perfect world, before it was swallowed
up: he was its little prince. He was the youngest of his mother's
four children, her baby and her favourite – he seems very
certain of that. She was so busy with the running of the business that he had incredible freedom from any sort of supervi-
sion. It was a far from normal life for a child but in his memory
it was wonderful. His familiars were his nanny, Tončka, and
the chauffeur, Tinček; they let him do whatever he wanted, or
so he describes it, and he slipped everywhere amongst the
guests. There is a picture of him at this stage, a bright-eyed,
handsome, and bold little boy in lederhosen. He partook of
anything he wanted to try, sipping champagne if it was offered
to him, and sitting at the terrace café and making people laugh
with droll stories, as well as playing on the lake and in the
pool. He made friends with the guests and their children and

his tales are full of titled people, his close friend Princess Doris especially, who was his age, but also Baroness This and old Count That.

He had no responsibilities at all, not even for his dog, Pooki, who was fed and cleaned up after by servants. This detail makes me uneasy. I question why he would not want to care for his own pet, having always assumed that enjoying doing so was part of why a person wanted an animal and was what helped create a bond. He just laughs at me. Such chores were servants' work. He was so indulged that when he was in his first term at boarding school, and homesick, he would let tears fall onto the pages of his letters home. The tear-watered writing had the happy result (and amazing to me who would never have expected such an outcome myself if I confessed the extent of my own homesickness) of his father coming to stay in the nearby village so he could visit him every day, to assuage his grief.

Frank's father was a good-looking, athletic man, though tending to plumpness in middle-age as I see in a later snap that is out of order in the pile. He did what his wife told him to do, or so I understand from what his son says. She is the one who built the Grand Hotel and who ran it. He, Sasha Molnar, had been in the Hungarian Cavalry in the First World War and had come into Slovenia with his regiment and there met the young Jula Vovk, whom he returned to marry after the war. I look at a photograph that shows them on their wedding day, he in his uniform, handsome and stern-faced (but as if he is holding the expression on purpose and would really like to smile) and she, also serious but more decidedly so, and there is something in her expression that feels familiar, an intentness. Innocence and intelligence are in her face, and also perhaps a strong will. A further picture of Sasha is one taken earlier: he is standing beside a road not in his dress uniform but in what I take to be battle dress and he gazes off to the side, not knowing the picture is being taken. He looks preoccupied and grim and handsome in a way that makes me know at once why she married him. Another interesting detail about him is that he ran in an early Olympics for Austria-Hungary.

Eden ended one fall day when Frank was eleven, home from his school for the weekend and cycling back after a day out. He was almost at Bled again, with only a few miles to go, and pedalling into Lesce-Bled. This was a tiny place, barely a village, where there was a "halt" for the train. He was just approaching the crossroads when he saw people lying on the road, five people. They were not in a row, as they would be if there were some purpose to their lying there, though what purpose could there be. They were in a disorderly clutter, a clutter of people. He remembered thinking, how odd. It's as if they were things: a couple side by side, a couple with one half-lying across the other, one body on its own a little distance away.

He cycled up and stopped and saw what he'd really known from the start but had tried not to know. They were all dead.

Blood had leaked out of them and was dark and sticky-looking around their heads.

No one else was anywhere about. It was a quiet scene, empty of life.

So that was how it began, the Germans in their midst.

His brother Miha was fifteen and wild to be part of the resistance. Their mother said to wait but he could not pay attention to her and he ran away one day and found the Partisans, joining them in their perilous work of bombing the trains that carried German troops and equipment. Unfortunately for him, the Communist Partisans soon sniffed out that he was a bourgeois boy, expendable. Thus they put him into the way of the greatest danger, and he, not seeing that the enemy was with him as well as against him, was brave and willing. But he was soon caught by the Gestapo. And that essentially was the end of him. It wasn't the end of him physically, but the man who came home from Belsen at the end of the war was not someone anyone in the family could recognize or reach. The most they learned was that he had spent his four-year imprisonment working cleaning up in the gas chambers. Finally freed, he spent a brief and silent period at home and then disappeared to Australia.

For his part, Frank did what he could by organizing an anti-Nazi underground at his school. This was soon uncovered with the result that he was hauled off to prison for three months, after which he was banned from all schools in "Greater Germany." That imprisonment was not bad, he said, not like a concentration camp and he was only thirteen, so much younger than the other prisoners that they made a pet of him. He was their mascot and he joked and lifted people's spirits. When he was released, since he could not return to school, his father took him up into the mountains and they skied.

Not long after the war was over, the Grand Hotel was nationalized. Twice more Frank was imprisoned, once with his father, once on his own. Both these times the jailers were their own Communist countrymen and there were no jokes. The oldest brother, another Sasha, an Olympic skier, escaped over the mountains on his skis, into Austria and thence to Switzerland. Frank returned to school, and then went on to the University of Ljubljana where he studied biology. He did well and that is what made it possible for him to secure his first job in Canada, teaching science at Bishop's College School. He will return to that at summer's end.

These stories are recounted over many evenings. Listening to them, I enter his life and experience it too, vicariously of course, but so closely it is almost as though I were there. It is partly the room we are in, with the uncertain light of fire and candle, the knowledge of the night outside, the black lake, and the black-and-white pictures which I must peer at carefully, holding them close to the candle flame. Under cover of darkness, I am being let into a secret history. And we are indeed hiding here as no one is supposed to be in the Club at night. But the spell he is casting is even more to do with the way he, the teller of this tale, looks at me, or looks away.

And then he pushes me back and pins me down and kisses me, a moment I have been waiting for through all the telling. I have never had a man hold me like this and touch me and I want him to do it. I welcome his weight pinning me down against the old, pleasantly musty chintz pillows of the Club sofa. I relive these sensations many times over when I'm not with him. They amaze me. I haven't experienced such a feeling of connection, of physical connection. And I feel protective. He has been through so much, and his body and his sad history, both, claim me. It must mean I love him. Can a person love two people? It seems I can.

Mr. MacLennan gets a certain withdrawn and grumpy look on his face if I mention Frank at all, and Frank, for his part, refers to Mr. MacLennan as "that old chap" and thinks it's funny, even the little bit he knows about our friendship. He gives it no serious consideration whatever. Frank, despite his wartime boyhood and his sense of exile often does find things funny. He has a way of giving in to laughing, his face going pink and his whole body getting into it, that I like a lot. Mr. MacLennan is a more steadily serious person and I suspect he is serious in his minding about Frank. As for me, I have always been good at keeping certain things secret and separate from other people.

On my walk home from Emily's, or later when I come up from the lake after my swim, there is my old friend, and Frank recedes as Mr. MacLennan smiles that smile I love. "Hop in, Anne. Come for a ride."

Emily is aware of both men and is amused. I realize she's also concerned. She looks a question at me sometimes and I can tell she is on the verge of speaking. Which is worse, I suspect she may wonder, the far-too-old man, or the younger one who is all too clearly trouble. But she still respects my privacy and waits for me to speak.

※

Mrs. Virgin is staging an old-fashioned summer fair at her farm. The ostensible purpose is to raise money for the Library, and Emily and I are helping and we are working hard, but we are also having considerable fun over the preparations.

The farm is a place I have visited regularly all my life: it is just west of the pasture where I have spent so many hours and days and I just need to climb the rail fence, descend a steep bank of blueberries and young maples, and I am among the pampered Jerseys. They are butterscotch-coloured, large-eyed cows, smaller than the plainer black-and-white Holsteins other farmers in the area have, but they are prodigious milkers. According to another farmer I know, it is because they are fed so very richly, and on supplements, not just grass. At milking time, they wend their way down to their luxurious barn, which is painted red outside and sky blue inside and has a sawdust-covered floor, kept pristine-clean and raked twice daily, after each milking, into neat lines. They have piped classical music to soothe the cows' spirits as they are clamped into the milking machines. This is farming of an entirely different scale and type than, say, Grant LeBaron's, who has two cows of no particular breed and taught Chuck and me to milk, with our fingers, plink, plunk into an old bucket. I enjoy visiting the Virgins' barn and always have a good long stare at the bulls, whom I have never seen out of their cages. What hangs almost udder-like beneath them is strange enough, but even more compelling is the steady rage that crumples their brows. Their narrowed eyes glitter with it, and the darkness seething around their pens makes them a different order of being from the cows, with their large, mild eyes, and their girlish way of skittering into their stalls. Rings through the bulls' noses chain them to the bars. They hate anyone who goes by and stamp and bellow at me, straining against their chains.

The farmhouse itself is the prettiest in North Hatley, being very old, long and low, with a steep-pitched roof from which peer small-paned dormers, and it is entirely furnished in antiques that fit in as though they had grown in their places, old Quebec pine pieces, or things brought up from New England. Altogether, everything about the farm makes me feel as if I am a character in a book, Hardy perhaps, though a Wessex barn would never be so fancy.

For the fair, Emily and Mrs. Virgin decide to dress me up. We are making nosegays, tightly packed small bouquets of tiny flowers, tied within paper-lace doilies by silk ribbons, and I will walk among the crowd proffering these from a wide and shallow straw basket. I will be an old-fashioned girl, a nine-teenth-century farmer's daughter, or a shepherdess. I cannot possibly wear any of my normal clothes and the two women ponder this. I suggest, and then show them, a long, dark pink dress that Mother has just found for me which she thought would do for the Club dances that we always go to. It is high to my throat and comes down to my ankles and is sleeveless. They decide it will do, and Emily searches out an antique hoop – it is well over one hundred years old, she tells us – that she has had in her attic forever. My hair now is very short, clipped close to my head like a boy's, and curlier than ever, not at all an olden-day hairstyle, but they decide that cannot be helped.

On the day of the fair, they dress me up in Mrs. Virgin's bedroom, where I have never been before, and I am interested to see that she has a four-poster bed with a canopy. They apply some pale-pink lipstick, they settle my long full dress over the hoop and they hand me my basket with the first batch of nosegays. The hoop lifts the skirt just enough so that the ruffled pantaloons Emily found just last night show a little.

I look in the mirror: my eyes look large and very blue and my cheeks are flushed. My arms are long and slim and smooth and the way the dress is cut, my shoulders are bare too, right to my collarbones. Perhaps I am even beautiful. I can't help smiling at myself, at this image of a young girl in the glass. She is demure but she is something else. I see a possibility of mischief and I like that.

"You look absolutely enchanting," Emily says. "I wonder if both your boyfriends will be here!"

"Both?" Mrs. Virgin says — she knows about my Slav, as her husband takes a particular interest in him (Mr. Virgin is a benevolent man who likes to help someone he sees as disadvantaged in some way, in Frank's case as an immigrant) — but Emily just laughs.

Almost everybody comes. They mill about in the different walled gardens, carrying their teacups and eating their cucumber sandwiches, their scones and lemon tarts, most things made by Mrs. Virgin's cook, but Emily and I did the sandwiches. ("Careful, careful — a very sharp knife for the crusts! Otherwise the filling squishes out." We lick our fingers when it does.)

Everyone wants one of my nosegays.

I see Mrs. MacLennan first, but luckily she veers off in a different direction: she does not appear to have seen me, and she is wandering across to look over the wall at the barn when someone greets her and engages her in talk. I hear her plummy tones as she propounds some large point or other. Her loud and low voice, whenever I overhear it, makes everything she says sound extra-important. Also boring.

And there he is. He comes up to me where I stand by a row of hollyhocks and widens his eyes. "Who are you? Are you Bathsheba Everdene, or are you Tess?"

"Oh, Bathsheba, of course. I could never fall in love with Angel Clare."

"You look a very sweet farmer then," he says. And I guess because I am in costume, he feels freer himself — or freer of himself. We are not in "real life" for a moment — is that it? — and he takes my fingers in his hand, lifts them to his lips, and kisses them. It is the closest intimacy he has ever allowed himself with me. And his wife is in sight, albeit with her back turned at this moment.

"But who are you?" I ask. "You can't be Farmer Boldwood." I don't want even to consider he might be Boldwood, given his terrible end, especially as he does have a whiff of him. "Perhaps you will have to be Gabriel." But that is not fair either though in an opposite way: Gabriel is not married, and is also not way older than Bathsheba. Mr. MacLennan does not fit any of the roles. Though suddenly I know who is Sergeant Troy, with his flashing sword that sliced the air around her head. He can't come today however, as he has to work.

"I wish I could be Gabriel," he says. "He gets her in the end. But" – and he says my thought himself – "I am far too old."

I flash him a look, "No. You aren't too old."

He lets go of my fingers, which he has been holding all this time; I don't think anyone has noticed, or would think anything if they did. I am in costume; this is fooling. An older man, a sweet young girl, a little teasing. Except it's not.

I am suddenly upset with him. "Take a nosegay for your wife," I say, and hand him one. And watch his face close down as he turns away. Tears jump into my eyes and I blink them back.

My parents know of the evenings I spend with Frank, though not that on many of them we are alone in the supposedly shut-for-the-night Clubhouse. I can tell they think he is completely unsuitable – too old, and foreign. They never engage him in conversation so know nothing but those two obvious things. But I am such a good girl and so young for my age. Also there is my famously unbendable will. I suspect they do not want to get my back up about this. They choose to wait – or this is what I imagine – and count on the "romance" blowing over at summer's end, only a short time away. I overheard my mother on the phone to a friend of hers, answering a question (she'd never have brought it up herself): "Just a summer romance," she said in carefully amused tones. I know those tones of hers. I was angry, though I said nothing.

On many Sunday evenings in the summer there are band concerts in the park. Everybody goes, village people, Club people, even some French people. This summer, Frank and I go together, sometimes in my canoe. The English name Frank doesn't seem to suit him, and in fact it is new to him; his real, full one is Frančišek Celesči Marcus Molnar, which must always have been too much of a mouthful and until he came to Canada, he was Feri. Feri is a name a man has to slip sideways out from under as soon as he arrives here. Feri Molnar immediately became Frank.

This Sunday we are in my canoe, and we are not far offshore but enough so that we cannot be seen by the people in the park who are moving about, walking, greeting each other, dancing (the children), and laughing under the lights of the bandstand. The lake is smooth around us except where the brilliant paths of light are reflected, running towards us over the black silk surface.

I am sitting on the bottom of the canoe and I lean back against him and his knees are gripping me on either side under my arms so that I am very aware of him behind me. I watch the glinting drips of water as he balances his paddle across me.

I am also very aware of a man on the shore who stands looking up at the musicians. He stands there alone – is his wife somewhere amongst the crowd? I can't see her – and sometimes he looks out over the water as if he can see us but of course he can't. He is within the light and we are outside it.

How difficult it is to think of Mr. MacLennan's wife, the unalterable fact of her. I try never to look at her directly, so I can pretend I don't have to consider her. But – she is a person too and I cannot now utterly ignore that she exists, as I did so successfully when I was younger. I do see her from time to time and she is always pleasant to me, even if in her headmistressy way, which perhaps is the only way she knows how to be with a young person. I have no idea what she imagines about me, or if she imagines anything at all. She may well know nothing, or almost nothing, about the amount of time her husband and I spend together. I think that must be the case, or how would their marriage work at all? He'd not be likely to tell her. Emily would certainly not tell her. Before I went off to McGill, Mrs. MacLennan even asked me, one day in the library, if I would like her to speak on my behalf about joining her fraternity – she had been in one eons ago at some college in the States and it has a branch at McGill. Actually she called it a sorority, as I think they do in other places than McGill. (I wonder why the ones at McGill are referred to as if they are male? To pretend girls are as important as boys, I suppose.) I thanked her and said no: I did not want to join one. Fraternities, their exclusiveness and narrowing of possibilities, their cruelties, are entirely outside my view of the world I want to be in. But it was kind of her.

She is even more surprising to me, however, now, as a wife for him. Obviously I am much more aware of things sexual than I was when I was fourteen, even though I am still a virgin, and I cannot help reflecting occasionally on that side of things, for them. She is greyer and older-seeming than ever – I think there may be a further chin – and he is still so clearly in his prime. I think of those legs of his. And I will not picture intimacies taking place. I refuse even to torture myself by trying to, it is so repellent a thought. I banish it.

I am eighteen, but he has moved along too, oh relentless time, and is now forty-seven. I will never catch up.

But now something embarrassing is happening. I squirm.

It is John Bassett's birthday party and he is holding it at the Club. Everyone is invited and it is a costume party, though no one expects the old ladies or the stuffier men actually to don exotic disguise.

I am wearing my mother's dark blue satin "lounging pajamas," a costume standby in our family for anyone wanting to be some sort of generic Eastern princess, and my sisters have made up my eyes. I am still no sort of hand at makeup, as I never wear it, but for this event I want it. I look quite exotic, for me.

Mr. MacLennan comes as a boxer. His most recent novel, *Each Man's Son*, is about a boxer and likely that is why it is on his mind. His male characters tend to have a toughness, some, like the boxer, even a working-class background. Or like Paul in *Two Solitudes*, who is a mix, having a working-class mother, and who plays hockey, a rough sport. I think he admires such men who are different from himself so maybe that's why he wants to pretend for an evening he's manly in the way they are. From somewhere he has acquired boxing gloves and satin shorts and a boxer-type dressing gown, which hangs open to reveal his chest and stomach. He prances and bounces around, making feints with his gloves and looks quite sweet, even if a bit silly. I rather wish he were less bouncy, and yet I should be glad, when he is generally so self-contained. He is showing off, I am sure of that, as well he might, but he makes me shy with this public display.

But Mrs. MacLennan's costume is what is so horribly embarrassing. She is being "Little Bo Peep," and the effect is so wrong I can hardly bear to look. She is not someone who can possibly seem sweet or, even less, cute. There is even something that strikes me, if no one else: the hideous coincidence that it's an echo of what I was wearing at Mrs. Virgin's fair — my "girl with nosegays," her shepherdess. She is so very tall and heavy, and her peasant "frock" accentuates that strange low bosom and is short enough to display — the pantaloons? Can Emily possibly have lent her the same pantaloons? Can there be more than one pair in the village? Emily, you traitress! Yet, if she were asked, how could she have refused? Can Mrs. MacLennan and I be sharers of the same pair of old-fashioned underwear? Her body repels me and I violently reject a connection with it.

I am mortified, for him. How can he bear it? And how can he have let her come out like this? Did she insist and he could not stop her? I long to know, but we have never discussed her and never will.

One day we are standing together in the park, Mr. MacLennan and I. It is a Saturday morning and I am not going to the antique shop. Frank is working, giving a tennis lesson, and I will likely walk on to the Club and see him shortly.

We walk down towards the low cement wall that edges the park, below which is a bit of rocky beach and the lake, which is lightly ruffled today and very blue and sparkly. For some reason I look back behind us, and I see a pair of boys approaching the park from down the Capelton Road. "Oh, dear," I say, "there is that pathetic pair."

Mr. MacLennan looks too. "Do you know them?"

"No. Of course I don't." I say of course because they are obviously French boys. The French people who live in the village, and, in fact, not really in the village but out on the edge of it, are impossible to get to know, in my experience. There are a few exceptions: the Bonnevilles, who have the store; Yvonne, who has worked for our family, and her sister Madeleine who sometimes replaces her. But for the most part, the French people are a separate race. The children go to the French school, which doesn't look like a real school and is so small it has only the one teacher, and of course being Catholic, they have their own church, which is huge, though at least it is an ordinary shingle building and not as wildly out of scale as the mammoth stone churches most villages have. Katevale, for example, a village of one short street on the way to Magog, has a vast stone edifice that towers ludicrously over the tiny huddle of houses. I sometimes see the North Hatley priest walking alone, though always from a distance. I have always found him a rather sinister figure in his black *soutane*, unfriendly, perhaps downright grim of face, though maybe that is my imagination just because he gives me the shivers. The French children keep very much away from the English ones, and seem to scuttle into the background and melt away as one comes along and they are smaller and thinner, with dark, narrow faces and shadowed eyes, as if they don't eat enough or the right things.

When I was very young and just able to read, I used to see small announcements placed in front windows or on front doors down the Capelton Road that filled me with distress and alarm. They signalled horribly to any passer-by that there was a degree of nightmare unimaginable to me in the lives of the French people in our village. They were signs that said PAIN.

I never dared ask anybody for further information. The signs themselves were awful enough and I couldn't bear to know details of what might be taking place within each of those sad little houses and what the purpose was of putting up the announcements.

It was some time, I'm not sure how long, if it was as much as a year or even two, before the truth finally dawned on me: they were merely requests for bread delivery. But the way the French people were perceived, and the way they looked as well, fitted with my fearful supposition.

The two boys we see now and whom I see every once in a while, maybe two or three times a summer, seem to be manifestations of my earlier fears. They are bound together forever because one is in a wheelchair and the other pushes him. The seated boy has an extreme case of club feet and his legs above them are as thin and wasted as little twigs. My mother has expressed her compassion for these boys, trapped together, and her helpless anger at the needlessness of the situation. The crippled one ought to have had surgery as a baby, and had he done so, he would presumably now be walking normally.

Poverty and ignorance doubtless play a role but there seems to be a terrible acceptance of misfortune.

My mother's anger at such a state of passive acceptance is linked to something terrible that happened in our own family. Our dad has a sister, our Aunt Ruth, a mysterious person I have only met once, as she seems to dwell outside the light of family respectability and even love. She is the embodiment of all the ways a woman can go wrong, seemingly. In the quest I have been on for years now to discover what kind of woman I want to be myself, I have naturally wondered just what she has done to earn this position in the shadows but I haven't learned much. She has been reckless, marrying and divorcing more than once, that much I know. And I also know that she had a little boy, Douglas, our first cousin, who died tragically, soon after I was born. I have never even seen a picture of this cousin. He was nine when he died and he had been sadly neglected before that.

My mother shook her head and pursed her lips when she told of Douglas as a baby, his diapers unchanged for far too long, and Douglas as a bigger child, sent to be looked after by my grandmother and Aunt Hazel for a few days — while Aunt Ruth doubtless was off on some unmentionable exploits — and their sad dismay at the condition of the child and of the clothes that were sent with him, so worn and soiled. But his end was terrible and terribly unnecessary: he died in a French Catholic hospital in Montreal while the nuns prayed around his bed. My mother explained how the doctor would not operate on him to remove his appendix without the permission of his long-lost-track-of father. Only a father would do, if there was one alive anywhere in the world. (Or in the case of a wife needing surgery, a husband. She could not make such a decision on her own behalf.) That was the law in Quebec and it still is now in 1954. But it is the image of the nuns praying around the little boy's bed that especially infuriates my mother, because it symbolizes for her, I think, the notion that prayers make it all fine. And my Aunt Ruth comes in for some of the blame too. I think Mother imagines herself in the situation and feels she would not stand for it, and would snatch up her child and race for the Ontario border and a place where reason and sanity rather than the Catholic Church and old Napoleonic Law prevail.

I tell Mr. MacLennan some of this history and why I find the two trapped-together boys disturbing and of course he is sorry as he is a kind-hearted man, and he is quite struck by my childhood misunderstanding of those signs.

Mr. MacLennan's most famous book, *Two Solitudes*, is about the French and the English in this province, the two separate cultures, but I am not really sure how many French people he actually knows. The priest, as a person of some education, would likely be the only one in this village that he might know, but he doesn't. But the French people in this village are a far cry from the patrician family in his book.

One afternoon as we drive along, he asks me if I have brought with me to North Hatley a copy of the story I wrote for which I won a prize at McGill. I am pleased he noticed it — it was published in the university paper — and he has not mentioned it until now and nor have I. He says he wants to read it again. "Again." So he has read it once.

"It's very promising," he says, handing it back to me the day after I give him a copy. I notice that he has made a few marginal squiggles of correction or comment and I hope I can read his writing. I am unaccustomedly shy with him in this sudden new role in which he is critic of my writing. We have discussed everything under the sun for years and yet I have never shown him anything I have written, not even the stories I got prizes for at Havergal.

"You must keep on," he says. "You have talent and you must not let it go to waste. To have won that prize — and I know the judges and they are very exacting — to have won was an excellent accomplishment. But Anne, I fear for you: you are letting yourself be distracted." What is he talking about? Is this the nearest he can come to mentioning Frank? And surely he himself has been for years my biggest distraction.

He is falling more and more into this new controlling mode and I dislike it. Imagining him as my Master (shades of Jane) is one thing; that has been mostly a game. I will not stand for being bossed. I turn away from him and look out the window. We are heading up the hill towards the Virgins' farm and I watch to see if any of the cows are down by the fence.

"You should write every day." His voice has that tone.

"You must not ever let praise go to your head." And this seems especially unfair, as he has not let much praise pass his lips. "It is a long hard task, to become a writer. You may think it is just a matter of talent."

"I don't."

He pulls off the road into the spot where we can see through a gap in the trees right across the little valley to the pasture where we have walked together in the past.

"Let me tell you a story," he says. "When I applied for a Rhodes Scholarship, I was excited. I was excited that people even thought it worthwhile my applying for it, that my professors had that sort of ambition for me, or dream, really. They probably thought it damn improbable that I'd be in the serious running, and I knew I was just a young man from a town on the hinterland of nowhere, Halifax, and had no real hope of winning. How could my background stand up against all the other brilliant chaps who'd be sending off their forms? It was a good exercise, I told myself. And I steeled myself to lose. I made an error, though, perhaps, in that I told my father. My father was a Calvinist, very Puritan. 'Don't expect anything,' he said to me. 'You'll not get it. Why should you? Think of all the other fellows who are applying and what they likely have to offer.' That was the gist of it.

"Well, time passed; ages passed, it felt to me. I knew I'd not won and it was a bitter feeling. I wished no one had ever mentioned it to me. And then, one fine, late winter day – the letter came. I opened it, entirely anticipating that it was merely to inform me I'd lost out. Well, I hadn't lost out. I'd won the thing. I was going to Oxford. I was going out into the world. I was going where all the greatest minds had been. Anne, I felt exultant.

"Then, my father came into the hall. He took the letter from my hand and read it, and then he stood there – oh, for about a minute. Then he said: 'Hugh, this is splendid news. I am very proud of you.' And then he let a further minute pass during which I suppose I just grinned at him. At that point I guess he figured we'd had enough of that: 'Hugh,' he said to me, 'get your boots on, and out you go. Shovel the snow.' There'd been a pile of new snowfall in the night."

"And that was it? That was all the pleasure you were allowed to get out of it?"

"Well, I already said, he was a Calvinist. I'd had my moment savouring my triumph and enough was enough."

"I hate that story!"

"No, no. He was right." He frowns at me. "You are extremely clever, Anne, and you are talented too. But sometimes you may be a little too proud, a little too certain. I fear that for you." First it was that I am distracted; now I am too big for my boots.

I stare back at him.

What is this really about? Is it personal? Is he criticizing me because he sees me straying away from his influence? Or is it more general, and related to all that business of women's power that he has been going on about lately, the cycle that is supposedly about to overtake us? I don't see it myself, but would not mind a bit if it did happen.

Or maybe the two things are really the same. He's afraid, is what it is. I'm an example, and one that really matters to him, of what is causing disruption in the world. He has always seen the patterns through which history moves and evolves, is set back, or advances. He believes vehemently in an almost medieval hierarchy, what we heard so much about in Professor Duthie's classes on Shakespeare this past year, and that as the old power structure weakens, as people overturn it, everything is imperilled. Women must not usurp men's power; I must not threaten his.

But I will. I have every intention of being as clever as I can, cleverer than he is, perhaps.

"I'm walking home," I say. There's no fighting him when he's in this mood, but I won't listen, either. I open the door and jump out, climb the fence, and am soon out of sight of the car. I don't look back.

I scramble down through the bushes, and it's very over-grown here. Brambles claw at my bare arms and legs so that I am soon smeared with blood, and I am hot with resentment. I wish I'd never shown him my story.

I climb the steep hill across the valley and I calm down and feel sorry. He wants the best for me, I know that, and he does not want me to court disappointment. I think of him driving off, and I hope he has indeed done so, and is not still sitting there, upset with me. I plan how I will be good to him tomorrow.

This summer we discover that my father has written a memoir, or a sort of memoir: it is tantalizingly elliptical but he has made it quite clear that he is not willing to elaborate. He is a wonderful teller of tales about his African adventures and his prospecting explorations in the Canadian Far North and in South America. His boyhood, though, seems to be locked inside him. This is quite different from our mother, whose childhood feels almost like an extension of my own, she has described things so well and so often. But she was a cherished little girl, not forced to be too responsible too soon as he was.

The surprising thing we find out in this piece of my father's is that both his parents were at Bishop's University. The University is only ten miles from North Hatley and Carol went there for a year before she entered nursing training, and much earlier, our mother's older brother, Edward, got his B.A. there, before entering McGill to do law, a plan fatally interrupted only a year or two along by the First World War. I have pored over photographs of handsome Edward, who seemed to have been on every possible sports team and looked very darling indeed in his striped sweaters and shorts, an impression poignantly enhanced for me by my knowing of death waiting in the wings to snatch him, and soon. My brother will likely go to Bishop's College School, in the same small town, and may well follow Carol to the University there. But the few details we do find hint rather forcefully at why our grandparents' having gone there too has never been mentioned before and is glossed swiftly over now.

My grandmother, Ruth Auburn, was eighteen when she arrived at Bishop's in September, 1898. She would have stepped across the same green lawns, entered the same red-brick, vine-covered buildings, as I have done when visiting there. Perhaps she lingered in the Cloisters or sat on the grass of the quad; she would have walked over the bridge into Lennoxville under the same huge trees, brilliant in autumn. Did she board in town? Were there residences for women then? These details are not included in our dad's brief account.

When I study now the two pictures we have of her I can see that she is rather lovely. I used to think she just seemed sad. She has thickly curling brown hair, like all her granddaughters, but in her case worn long and pinned up. Her eyes are large and I imagine them as the same bright blue as my dad's, and they are tilted down a little at the outside corners. It is a set of eye that can easily be sad, and hers are. She has a strong nose, high-bridged, and full lips, like my dad's, like mine.

She had graduated from the High School of Montreal, winning the gold medal for being the top-ranking student of her year, and then entered medicine at Bishop's, the only one of the seven children in her family to go on to university. Her goal was to be a dentist. I don't know when Bishop's ceased to have a medical school; it certainly doesn't have one now.

Perhaps it's because I am eighteen now, the same age she was then, and have just finished my own first year of university, that I find my imagination playing around the image of this grandmother, and wondering if she was like me in more than a few of her physical features. That she died long before I was born means she can exist for me as a girl, without the disturbance of other memories getting in the way, and I can imagine her as I will. I identify with her as I picture her arriving in Lennoxville, full of excited expectations, and proud of her achievements to that point: she must have worked hard and been extremely keen and clever to have got herself into medical school.

But then: disaster. Her academic ambitions all came to nothing. Before the first Christmas holiday that would have ended her first term, she was gone. She eloped with my grandfather, Thomas. He was thirty-five, almost twice her age, and he was her professor. How did this come about, I wonder, thinking of course of my own impossible love. My father's writing of these events is so infuriatingly spare that I cannot even be sure if she was pregnant at the time they fled Bishop's. That Thomas, a professor in the medical faculty, left his position, suggests she was. Why otherwise would he take such a drastic step, and I do know that in fact there was an earlier baby boy who died before my father himself was born. If she were indeed pregnant, my grandmother must certainly have been more sexually bold than I. But I wonder if her feelings might have started in the same way as mine for Mr. MacLennan. Something about his face or his hands, say, caught her romantic imagination and that, combined with the facts of his intelligence and knowledge in the field she wanted to enter and his power over her, fired a passion in her. I picture her haunting the corridor outside his office, perhaps falling into a habit of hanging behind after a lecture with a question. I see her lying awake in her bed at night, fantasizing. As I have done myself.

Or perhaps it was not a bit like that. I send my imagination down a very different path. Perhaps my grandfather was not nearly the honourable man that Mr. MacLennan is.

Her professor is the predator: she enters his office. It is dim and wood-panelled. There is a tall small-paned window overlooking a lawn that is covered with yellow leaves. He stands by his desk, and with the window behind him, she cannot make out his expression. She holds out her assignment. Which he does not take. Instead – he grabs her wrist and pulls her towards him. What does she feel? Shock? Yes. But then, fear? Delight? I identify with her and I suspect she does not feel delight, no, not delight. I put myself in her place and it is a sense of fatedness I feel. This is the thing that must happen, the thing I deserve. How did I think I could get away with this, with being so clever, with having aimed so high?

My father writes very little about this grandfather, his own father, and he moves in his memoir around and behind this figure, whom he leaves as a block of shadow. We do know already from our mother that our dad's childhood was unhappy, that his father died when he was only eleven and had not been a pleasant or kind man even while he was on the scene. She has told us of one terrible occasion when, as a little boy, to protect his younger sister, he took the blame for something she had done. His father soaked his belt in salt overnight and used it to beat our father-to-be. The purpose of the salt was to cause even more pain when the skin broke under the cruel blows. This degree of calculated brutality and sadism chilled us. The few pictures of my father as a child make it even worse to imagine. In them, he is a skinny little boy, with his mother's same sad eyes, though they never meet the camera. He looks away and doesn't smile. Our mother blames our grandmother as well as our grandfather for the beating: she should have managed to stop him. We don't know how our father feels about this now — what his father did, how his mother failed to protect him — as he's never spoken of it and there are few details about his father in the memoir and very few about his mother. He does throw light on the more estimable Coleman forebears. For example, he is proud of the first Thomas Coleman, who was born in England in 1787 and came to Belleville, Ontario, as a United Empire Loyalist. There he made his fortune. He became a colonel in the War of 1812, raising a regiment to fight alongside his friend, the Indian Tecumseh. And after him there is one after another of Thomases and Charleses, all doctors or lawyers. They live, in their turn, in the enormous, Italianate "Coleman's Castle" that one of them builds, and which we were once taken to see in its current role as a funeral home. These are the ancestors he chooses to claim for us.

His female relatives are people my father apparently is uncomfortable speaking about for reasons that are never explained. Sometimes I get a sense that he fears lest any of his daughters follow in their – misguided? immodest? unhappy? – footsteps and that seems to mean we must know little about them as if we could be contaminated by such knowledge. Or it could just be that it hurts him to talk about their sad histories.

He is very careful not to indulge us too much, which is not especially logical in that I don't think either of the erring (if in fact my grandmother was erring) women was indulged in her day, my grandmother having been one of seven children, and my Aunt Ruth growing up in the same straitened circumstances as my father, after their father died. But it certainly seems the case that neither of the women was sensible and practical about raising children on her own, which both of them had to do. And here is where I very definitely take a lesson: if I am on my own with children, after that flight I picture so vividly, I will manage far differently and better than my grandmother and my aunt. I will be a mother-tiger-woman like my own mother and my children will not suffer. But any "lesson" I take from my father is muddled. He has been heroic, exploring the wild parts of the world – Africa, the Andes, the Far North – but even though he likes it that I am brave, it is always somehow made clear that his kind of work is not a possibility for a girl. My father used to take pleasure in our doing math together. He didn't move ahead of me when we did it. He liked to see that I could find my own way, and I always did. I was the only one of his children who loved it as he did. But I have lost math now. That is a sad knowledge that I can't ever bear to address in my mind and so I push it away. It feels as if certain possibilities and strengths can slip away like mist, or smoke, when someone isn't paying proper attention. What other things am I losing, without noticing? Sometimes I worry.

There has been a pattern in my family whereby clever women trip and fall. I wonder if I may fall, in my turn, and if I do, if I will be able to pick myself up and run on. Somehow I must.

One small mystery is cleared up by my mother, when we ask her for some explanation, at last, about the odd connection of our family with Joe Sampson, the rather surly, growzly owner of the pasture I consider to be my own private territory. We find the story both interesting and even funny, my sisters and I, but my father is not there when mother tells us, as it is one of those chapters that make him uneasy. He is so honest I guess he hates to acknowledge a connection with people who are not, even though the misdeed had nothing to do with him, or in this case, not even with a blood relation.

My grandmother's sister Emily, known as Aunt Emmy, was rich, or appeared to be. She lived in a large house on the side of the mountain in Montreal, and she was the person with whom my dad stayed as a child here in North Hatley. She owned, or would rent, houses here: a place way down the lake past Black Point that they would get to by boat (a rowboat, in those days), called Saint's Rest, or sometimes a large red cottage up behind ours, just below the pasture. In our childhood, she had a lover, Mr. Fraser, who lived with her in her Montreal mansion (I remember him: he looked just like Jeremy Fisher, the gentlemanly frog in Beatrix Potter's tale of pond life, and was jolly to us.) Sex being part of the story – however hard for us to imagine, our beautiful great-aunt and that frog-person – is one reason for my father's discomfort, though he loved his aunt. Mr. Fraser used to send us a big, fancy tin pail of hard candies at Christmas – a present that was always spirited away by mother before we had so much as tasted them. But how she got her money is the really interesting part. It happened this way: she married a man called McNeil – the father of my dad's McNeil cousins, but a man never seen by us, as she had somehow shaken him loose. He was a drinker. However, his money stuck to Aunt Emmy. How, is left shady. The money, though, was shady already: back in the last century, the father of Aunt Emmy's drunken husband was a bank manager down in New England, just across the border in Vermont somewhere. One fine day, he scooped up all the cash in his care, and with his wife, and perhaps his son, though we don't know if he was born yet, he slipped across the border and fetched up in North Hatley. He bought a farmhouse up on the Minton Road, several miles from the village. He had a special addition constructed, a secret section of the house, where he could hide out if the law came looking for him. The law never did. The ill-gotten gains stayed in the McNeil hands, and then in Aunt Emmy's. The drunken husband's sister married old Joe. So there we were!

And the house with the secret hiding place is now where Mrs. Virgin's herdsman lives. I like the tidiness of that: I even know the house, though have never seen the secret part as I've never been inside.

When I was a child, adult sex was one of a number of strange and never openly referred to things about the world of grown-ups. It seemed entirely unrelated to certain behaviour of my small group of boys and girls. Suddenly on a summer afternoon, a small whirlwind would nip in from somewhere and spin us into guilty excitement. There would be whispering, and then a race off to the woods for what we called Silly Time, or

S.T., for short. There was a deeply thrilling feeling during those moments as we ran, but always more promise in the anticipation than in the actual events that followed, which never quite lived up to whatever we'd thought they'd be like this time. We would seek a dim and leafy spot, take our clothes off, and peek at each other. We all, boys as well as girls, seemed equally silly, equally naughty. The silliness and naughtiness were the point, and keeping what we were up to secret from our parents. Our behaviour seemed to have nothing to do with anything adults themselves might be likely to do. Since then, any such feelings and experiments have become more private for us all and for me have found outlet, until I met Frank, simply in daydreams.

I am aware of how adults, some adults, use sex. Men can use sex as a weapon: the excitement and fun arise from forcing it upon some weaker and even unwilling person. She, at least while a man is exerting his power over her, does not seem to exist as a person for him. I think I can't have existed as a person for Patsy's father.

But women use sex too, even if more as a tool than a weapon, though I'm not sure exactly what the difference is as both are about use. I know this from my days of listening to the Club women's conversations, and I still observe it: sex is withheld or given to achieve something. A new mahogany dining-room table, perhaps, or a fur coat. Or it can be dishonest, a trick.

I heard one day the mother of a friend of mine telling the other women how she forced herself to wake very, very early every morning, in order to slip into the bathroom and apply her makeup before her new young husband awoke. He must never, ever see her naked face. I ponder now how this fits into my picture. The woman was engaged in pathetic trickery and surely one day she would be caught out, the crinkled skin around her eyes glimpsed. And presumably that happened one lazy, unvigilant day, as by the next summer he had left her. But when she told of her ploy, while he was still with her, she was laughing. She saw it as clever — or did she? I didn't understand and still don't.

I am determined not to play a part myself in this sort of dishonesty and I know not everyone is like that. My own parents surely are not, nor is Mr. MacLennan, whatever his odd marriage is built on. Frank is not like that either, as far as I know, but there is something manipulative about him that is disquieting if I let myself think about it.

And all about me are men. There have always been men about, of course, but now I am more curious and bothered by the way they can be so different from each other and from women. There are nice ones and not nice ones — like Patsy's father — and there are others who seem nice and then suddenly show a different self and leer or fondle. I can't figure out why they want to push themselves on someone who is unwilling.

Where can the pleasure be? And yet many of my friends have had the same experiences I have had, and for at least two of them the fondlers have been their own fathers, which would surely be the worst of nightmares.

I have another very specific memory of Patsy's father that I cannot place for certain and that haunts me now for some reason, I guess because of this new preoccupation I have with the baffling quality of men.

In the memory I am fifteen I think, or at least no older than sixteen. I am sure that I am still a schoolgirl, not someone heading off to university, as I was the summer I was seventeen. It is a horrible memory but it has a calm ending.

That man: he has lurked all along in the wings of my life but at the time of this memory, I think I haven't seen him for a while. Patsy and I have even less in common than before, when I moved ahead into other reading. She too has moved on to other things and our chief conversational topics have died. However, that family is still about, and one night I encounter him, her father.

I am returning to collect my canoe after visiting another friend on that side of the lake, the Club side, so I have beached it there. It is starting to be dusk, being the end of the summer and the evenings drawing in, and in fact in a couple of days we are heading back to Toronto. I am looking forward to what may be the last paddle of the summer across the lake as darkness falls. I love the water at this time of end-of-day and especially the stillness, broken only by the small noise of my paddle and maybe a child calling, some small person who doesn't want to go to bed, a sound that echoes across the water, and the last of the light catches the ripples I make as I sink my paddle into the surface of this element I am floating upon. It is cool, the beginning almost of fall.

But as I cross the sand, which is cold under my feet, it being too late in the season for sand to hold the sun's warmth after it has slipped from the sky, I hear a voice:

"Anne, could you come and help me for a minute?"

It is Patsy's father and the very last thing I want is to help him, even to see him. I turn. "What is it?" I ask.

"Just help me for a second. I need to collect two sails from the locker and I'm in a hurry – I can't carry both at once – can you come and take one of them?" Even as he speaks, he is mounting the stairs, taking for granted I will follow. I have had nothing to do with this man for maybe two years, and I think a whole confusion of things: I must be polite; it is silly to think he'll even remember those old stupid grabbings that happened ages ago; if he tries anything, I'll kick him between his legs. Someone, Carol in fact, has told me to do this. Mysteriously, a kick between a man's legs will halt him in his tracks. He'll maybe even fall down and groan.

Resignedly, I follow him up the stairs. It is really dark as the light that is still in the sky outdoors does not penetrate here, where the dormer window is tiny and the walls are unpainted old wood. I can barely make out where he is.

But he can see me better, I guess because of my white blouse and shorts, and a second after I step into the room, he grabs. And there is no room to aim a kick — that was useless advice for this occasion anyway — and he holds me firmly against him with one heavy arm and this man is so huge I am instantly terrified. I have no power in this situation, I know it. I am done for. And his other hand shoves itself up my thigh, works itself up, sort of in steps, as if he is enjoying — well, I guess he is enjoying — getting closer and closer to the top of my leg so he can get his fingers inside my shorts. Which he starts to do.

His fingers are right up at the edge of my underpants, almost slipping under their elastic edge, when I truly start to fight back. What was wrong with me before? And maybe it's also his stupid excitement that undoes him — I think it must be — because he leans back and laughs, as if this might be something we both are enjoying. And that gives me my chance.

I summon all my strength and I heave him back away from me. I think he is so excited he doesn't know what I am doing at first. And I run. I race down those stairs and I scream something back at him, I don't know what.

I am across the beach and shoving my canoe out before he makes it to the bottom of the stairs and I am very glad I am swift and strong. I am not as strong as he is of course, but I can run, and I do run.

He stands on the sand and calls after me, "Anne, Anne, I didn't mean any harm! You didn't have to run away." But he did mean harm and we both know it.

When I arrive at the other side of the lake I stop just out from our boathouse and find myself crying from the shock of it. The wild heart-pumping power that enabled me to escape has subsided, and I sit with my paddle across my knees and breathe and breathe the cool, fresh night air, and say to myself, It's okay, Anne. It's okay.

Then I hear talking at the boathouse: my brother and David Pollock are there, so I pick up my paddle again and go and join them. They want to swim and we do, but I don't tell them what has happened and I go out by myself very far, swimming quietly, sensing the depths below me and letting the water smooth away what has happened, or trying to. I find the memory is still thumping inside me later on when I'm in bed and each time I almost drop into sleep, I feel his terrible, probing hands.

The next day, I see Mr. MacLennan. Of course I don't tell him about the sail-locker horrible thing, but I sit quietly with him in a way I don't usually do and I think he knows something is wrong, that something has happened to upset me. He doesn't ask me about it in any direct way but when he stops his car so I can get out, he says — and I don't know how he knows to say it, that I need to hear it — "Anne, I am always someone who is on your side. I care about you." I don't know that he even knows what he means himself, but I feel safe again. The sail-locker event recedes.

He may actually have had in his mind something quite different, not triggered by my silence at all. Perhaps he didn't even notice it. We are both so reticent about what our friendship means. I never know how much of it is something I am making up and reading into the situation. I can't be doing that entirely. But what I mean to him, how he thinks about me – if he even does when I am not with him – all of that is unfathomable to me.

✗○

My memories take on a life of their own and I let them. I want to discover what I unconsciously pushed aside as I moved along my path. What were the things that snuck past the barriers with which I attempted to protect myself? There was a process happening that is mysterious to me still. I was trying to keep my essential self free and clear. Yet for a while I lost it, for all my striving. How did I? There were confusing messages from my father and my mother, my sisters. So many things were said or implied, and they had built-in contradictions. And how did Mr. MacLennan fit in with all the rest of what was shaping me?

For almost the whole of my second and third years at McGill, Mr. MacLennan slipped to the background of my life. He was still there, a resonating figure, but offstage. I didn't think of his missing me, or thinking of me, really, and for my part it was as if I knew that when our paths would cross, my emotion about him would come into full life again. It was like music turned right down, but the record player still on, a murmur. Of course I followed what he wrote, and read his articles — travel articles sometimes, or "occasional" essays — and I reread his books. Doing that, I would think to myself, I know this person, but it would scarcely seem possible; the man I'd sat beside in his car, the man who had once taken my hand, he had to be someone else. During that period, I had one entire summer in Europe, never getting to North Hatley at all, and another summer of minding children while their parents were in Europe. I didn't arrive home until well along in August that year. But over the couple of weeks left of summer, I did see Mr. MacLennan and it was as it had ever been. We talked, and I watched his face as he watched me, and I tried to guess what he was really thinking.

And there was still, and increasingly, Frank. I tried once, during my second year at McGill, to break off from him. He was teaching again at Bishop's College School, in Lennoxville, and he'd come into Montreal for weekends sometimes, then more often. I began to feel emotionally cornered, restless at his intrusion into my McGill world, the freedom of which seemed an entity unto itself. My friends found him intriguing and glamorous, which was a seductive realization. As time passed, his humour, which had gone some way to balancing his darker moods, seemed to be less in evidence and he became very possessive. Finally I got sick of the intense look on his face; it made me want to be cruel. I told him not to come again. But then I met him one day during the Christmas holidays, skiing. The look of him, hatless, in his casual khaki pants and black turtleneck (though he was an aristocrat as to equipment and had the best, most expensive European kind), so swift and full of grace on his skis, a dark bird in flight, undid my resolve. We sat in the little inn pub afterwards and he massaged my freezing feet and I was caught again. After that, I would not be able to extricate myself. He made it too clear he would die if I did. Die! The power it seemed to give me was frightening, but I couldn't resist it.

ALMOST

This is going to be an exacting day and I hope I can cope with it. I am challenged even on the purely physical level, which is humbling for someone as normally sturdy as I am. I find myself sitting and having a few self-pitying tears because I can't muster the strength to walk up the hill to the gym. It's even a little scary. Nothing like this bodily betrayal has happened to me before and it's probably a good lesson in what feebleness is like and how poor I seem to be at contending with it. And I am finding that physical weakness makes me more vulnerable emotionally.

I'm not even seriously sick, though I briefly thought I might be. It's bad timing though, to have had to have my appendix out just one week before my fourth-year final exams, and now, I, who have wanted so badly to do brilliantly in Mr.

MacLennan's class and am at long last taking a course of his, am wondering how in the world I'm to totter up the hill to the gym to write the exam.

I was allowed to write my "Russian History, the Revolution and After" exam in the residence infirmary, the nurse invigilating, which felt very peculiar at first. I sat on a small white chair at a little white table that had appeared from somewhere, and by a tightly made-up bed, and I flexed my fingers and wondered how I was going to be able to take this seriously (hearing nursely bustlings in the background didn't help). But as soon as I plunged into the first question, I entered that state of tranced exhilaration that comes as soon as I begin writing an exam, when I at once pass into some other cool element where I am floating and everything is clear and white and silent. I adore exams, not that a person can say that aloud. I wonder how many people actually love them and also don't dare say so, for fear of being too infuriating, as most people obviously loathe them and get into a state of nerves and panic that is sad to see, and from within which they definitely would not care to hear of others' enjoyment.

Even while I was still in the hospital, I had my French oral. The professor – thin, young, not much older than I, and so very much the intellectual as to seem of another, bloodless species – chugged up the hill himself and sat by my bed while I did my best to hold forth intelligently. According to the rules, I chose my two questions from the slips of paper laid, upside down, on my tray. Every few minutes, mid-thought, I had to close my eyes and wince as gas pains moved agonizingly around deep inside me. I could not possibly mention them and I was terrified they would result in wind escaping. This young man would very likely faint dead away if a girl, or anyone for that matter, behaved in such a revoltingly animal manner.

But for this English exam, "English Prose from Bacon to the Present," it is imperative that I make it up to the gym, if I have to crawl on my hands and knees: I must see Mr. MacLennan, even if from afar and even if there is no possibility of speaking to him. He won't invigilate, himself, and he may not even come, under the circumstances. But I want to be there, if he does. It's him I am so upset about.

Something terrible has just happened to him. My friend Sonya heard it on the news last night.

Sonya comes in the door even as I think of her. She has been taking the course too and we've always walked to class together, sat together in the front row, and walked home across the campus through the darkness — it is a late afternoon class — to Royal Victoria College, our residence, talking about what Mr. MacLennan has just said and analyzing every detail of how he said it and every expression that crossed his face and what it might mean. She is the only person in the class — which is large — who is aware that he and I are friends. Certainly neither he nor I has betrayed our relationship in any way. We are completely formal and he calls me Miss Coleman. Of course I still call him Mr. MacLennan whether in class or out of it, and I can't imagine not doing so. After all these years of talking together an uncountable number of times, I have not advanced to his first name. Which is how I like it. I remember how I used to be Jane, in my mind, and he, Mr. Rochester, or my Master. And there is something still between us that smacks of that, a formality that heightens whatever it is between us, which I still can't really define. But definitely it is secret (except from Sonya) and both the secrecy and the formality sharpen it.

"Sonya," I say, "I don't think I can walk up there. I feel awful — yet I have to go. I have to! And when I think of even getting along to the corner of University and Sherbrooke, I start to cry again. What am I going to do?" Weak tears fill my eyes.

I can't stand this feeble way I'm being, it's much too embarrassing, and one of the worst aspects of it seems to be the inability to see solutions even to trivial problems, because Sonya says quite calmly, "I've called a taxi. Come on. Got your pens?"

We descend the stairs together and head outdoors where we stand on the pavement waiting for the cab. It is a warm day in early May and Montreal has rushed from late winter the week before, everything dusty, brown, and dreary, into burgeoning buds and almost summery, humid air. I missed the day or so of brief transition while I was incarcerated inside Royal Victoria Hospital and now we are in spring. It has rained in the night and we have a moist, uncertain morning, the sky still clouded, the sidewalk wet and black and spotted with the bright yellow-green of fallen leaf-flowers, and the smells of earth, and new green growth sharp in the air.

Sonya Ignatieff is as tall as I am and also slim. She has an English voice and a dramatic manner and her stork of a father — six-foot-six, the tallest man I've ever met — was a Russian émigré who fled as a child, with his brothers and his English nanny, before the guns of the Bolsheviks. The south of France, Paris, London (where he married and had a daughter) were temporary perches before he took final flight and alighted in Canada when Sonya was thirteen. I like this background in my friend, that she is a descendant of princes and counts, not for snobbish reasons but just for its interesting historical echoes and the small connection it allows me with Tolstoy's world.

I have studied all the Eastern European history courses McGill has to offer, even travelling down such byways as "Eastern European Methods of War" (requiring reading volume after volume of Clausewitz), and a half-course on "The History of the Hapsburgs." I have taken a course on Islam. What I will do with my oddly chosen patchwork quilt of knowledge after I graduate is hazy to me. I have no thought of a career. I will marry; I will have children. None of my group ever speaks of working or having a career. Sometimes we play with the idea that in some misty future we will find ourselves writers, or artists. We are all both clever and energetic, but we accept, without even thinking it out, that only men, at this stage, have futures out in the world. Sometimes this knowledge brings a gust of an emotion that I might almost call grief. It is a grey recognition of . . . what? It's related to what I feel when something makes me remember my old joy in math and how I loved entering that cool, upland landscape – akin to where I go when writing exams – where pure logic lived. I lost the way to it by way of math in my first year at university. The teaching was so poor and I let it go. I allowed myself to be distracted by the girls who gossiped at the back of the classroom. The situation killed it, is all I can think now and that doesn't seem to be enough. Not at all enough. I thrust the topic away from me. It is too late, and I am good at keeping things in check. I wonder if my friends' minds shut off like this too, before such thoughts can form themselves into words. I have no way to open the subject. It is too huge and strange. But I have loved my time at McGill. My consciousness of that is very sharp, now that this precious and free period of my life is over.

However, a thick black curtain hangs between me and my future and I haven't the X-ray eyes to penetrate it in the smallest particular nor can I twitch a corner of it aside. I can say, "I will marry; I will have children," and in fact here there is a tiny twitching aside of the curtain after all for I can see those children and almost feel the weight of the first one in my arms, a dark-haired baby boy with his father's slightly slanted eyes. In my body I know him already. I mean in my body-imagination.

I am still a virgin and my baby is not within me yet. But soon he will be. Yet I cannot visualize, and cannot even try to, another single thing about the future my baby and I will inhabit.

I am following an inexorable trajectory, as I see it at this moment. My future is pulling me towards it with no will of mine being involved, except to will myself to have no will and no resistance. This is what is expected, I tell myself. I have to try to be normal. I will marry Frank and enter whatever waits for me behind that curtain. He will kill himself if I don't.

Meantime, I will take my exams.

As well as the history courses, I've done English every year and thus today, we are taxiing up the hill to write Mr. MacLennan's exam. I have done well in the course so far. I was leery of his marking my papers, fearing his eagle eye would catch silly errors (committed, and left in, from sheer nervousness or self-sabotage) and alter his opinion of me: too clever for her own good, but maybe, ah! not so clever after all. Or that he would fall into his superior-man mode: she may be good, but it had better not go to her head. But neither has happened and I have earned a string of As from him. He had his students go to his office with their final papers and read them to him, à la his Oxford tutorial days. I planned my outfit that day with extreme care, for reasons I'm not clear about since he has seen me from childhood in every state of careless dishevelment, but for that office session, I donned my crimson cashmere sweater, which is my nicest thing, and my beautiful and brilliantly patterned Liberty scarf, both items bought by Mother and me in London. My hair is long again now and I pinned it up in as high a bun as I could manage, though tendril-curls always straggle down a little.

I still feel my intense fascination. My heart jumps when I enter the classroom and see him there, as if each time I am surprised. The way he paces, or sits on a desk, the way he berates us all for knowing no history whatever (according to him) — all of this is so familiar to me and yet strange, here. He is different in any of our interactions on campus from the Mr. MacLennan of our past drives and talks. He is more serious and his clothes set him apart too from his scruffy North Hatley self, as here he wears a shirt and tie, a jacket, grey flannels. I have been self-conscious, if ever alone with him in his office, as I never was before, and I have no idea if he took in my effort at looking grown-up that day. He watched me in his thoughtful way and I read my paper. (It was on James Joyce's *A Portrait of the Artist as a Young Man*. I had loved writing it.) He commended it and took it from my hand to mark it, and I went away. I hoped at that point that he had not noticed my attempt to impress him with my beauty, as it made me feel foolish. I wished I'd gone in my knee socks and with my hair in a messy braid. Likely he wouldn't have noticed either way. I do still love him, I fear.

All the students sit waiting for their papers and I experience that enormous tension and excitement I always do when

I am on the brink of leaping off a high diving board, or, in this case, leaping into that airy dimension of creative thinking when my exam persona takes over. It is like flying once I begin.

However, there is more in my mind than that: I am hoping I can sustain my energy, in this queer post-operative state I am in, without suddenly having to put my head down on my booklet and give up.

But, over and above any other thing, I am full of anxiety for Mr. MacLennan. What Sonya heard on the radio this morning was that his wife died yesterday. I wonder just how devastated he will be. Very, I suspect. And I have heard that grief is exhausting, so there will be that too, on top of sadness, and she has been dying for ages so he has had all that long lead up to contend with as well, years of it really, but lately more awful, and now it has happened. There has been a lot of talk about how terrible this has been for him and while I can't pretend to grieve for her myself, given that I never knew her, I am very sad — for him.

For all my greater maturity now, I still do not have any idea of the way their marriage worked, how the dynamic between them operated. Given my entirely outside role, I never observed them together except briefly: her calling him away, his responding or not. But I do know she was his underpinning in some very significant way. I have hated to acknowledge it, jealous as I've always been, but he must have loved her and even if it was as a son, it would not matter, in terms of the strength of his dependency on her, indeed would maybe make the bond all the more powerful. I have speculated about them often of course, in the light of what I read, and even in the light of what my friends who have been taking psychology courses have discussed with me. We have often subjected ourselves, our families, and our friends to analysis, I making my points from my basis of literature and my friends from the new theories they are discovering.

It could be that he was the weaker person, that the domineering qualities that seemed so unappealing to me were the very qualities that he needed, despite his theories about the dangers of female power. And frail and ill as she may have been for decades, she may also have been his necessary prop and his caring for her a necessary sacrifice, meeting some self-denying need of his own. From the beginning, I sensed what I called shadows in him and over the years I have gradually developed a conviction that he has always been afraid to claim happiness for himself.

My Freudian friends, were I to discuss him with them — which I don't — would want to speculate about his relationship with his mother, so often, to them, source of all character dislocations. That is often too simplistic in my view, despite my liking *Sons and Lovers* so much, but I know nothing of his mother as he has never talked to me about her. (How significant, I can hear one of my friends exclaiming.) I have too fragmentary a picture of his early life to be certain of anything, and I bet that he isn't clear at all himself and that even inside his own head, reticence reigns on many thorny subjects and many lids are kept tightly clamped down. The best I can come up with as chief darkener of his spirit would be the weighty Scotch puritanism his father placed on his shoulders. Or more insidiously and powerfully than any direct placing on shoulders, the old doctor would have woven those lessons, by precept and example, into the very fabric of his son's mind, and of his body too.

Yes, his body too: I say that for more than one reason, but something that has always bothered me is the stiffness, even downright falseness of the sex scenes in his novels. Reading them, I am embarrassed for him. Other writers of the modern period are able to be quite explicit about sexuality. With Mr. MacLennan it's as if he feels obliged to bring it in from time to time, but there is no naturalness in his doing so and certainly no heat. I wonder about a connection between that reticence and self-consciousness on the page, and what his living sexuality might be.

However, these thoughts I have about him are only possible when he is not with me. When he is, I am so aware of him physically that what his feeling for me might be is obscured for me. I wonder if I can have such a strong response to him without his feeling something comparable and I don't know the answer. Of course I know that people can love unattainable people (as with me and Laurence Olivier ages ago) and that in such cases there is obviously no "relationship." The whole thing is entirely a fantasy. In our case though, there is a relationship and his feelings appear to be as strong as mine, but their nature is something I am forever at a loss to uncover.

If I am right that puritanical guilt was a mainspring of his marriage, what if she did know about me, and it hurt her? If that were so, he would feel guilty about it, and might have to turn his back on me.

The invigilator hands out our papers and eventually — it always feels long — we hear the words: "You may turn over your papers." Mr. MacLennan has not come in and I begin to write.

I enter what seems a timeless world, yet part of my mind is quite aware of time passing, and is punctilious about allowing for each question only its allotted number of minutes.

Two hours along, I stop to take a deep breath and a stretch, as much as I can stretch and not pop my stitches, about which I still feel apprehensive, as if a hasty movement or even a cough might rend them. How very ghastly it would be to have to stumble from the room clutching at my leaking insides, my brilliant paper unfinished. The huge room is silent except for the slight shiftings and occasional gusting sighs of various of the hundreds of students bowed low over their work. I gaze around and recognize no one. Many different classes write at the same time and my own classmates are either in front of me or behind me. To either side there are strangers, glum, intent.

One, at least, is excited: a tall, thin, rather spotty young man across from me smiles at whatever insight he is penning.

My heart jumps. Having concluded some time ago that he was not coming, I now see Mr. MacLennan at the far end of my row. He doesn't see me yet but he is walking towards me.

He is wearing his North Hatley clothes, his old blue sweater and his ancient jeans, and they make him my friend again, not the serious professor he has been in recent months. I am struck by how terribly familiar he looks, the only other real person in this great and otherwise entirely impersonal space, and his face is — what is it? I have never seen him look like this. It is shock, I conclude, pure and terrible shock. His eyes are wide and strained and blank as if he is not really seeing any of us. Sleepwalker's eyes, I think, though I have never looked into a sleepwalker's eyes. He continues to come towards me and I watch him and see the moment when he notices me. The sight of me stops him for a second, and seems to move him a little out of his shock to the point where he knows it is me. And he then continues walking, until he is right beside my desk. He looks directly at me: his eyes are very blue today, something that always happens when he wears this sweater. And then he smiles; he does fetch a smile from somewhere and he stands there by me and — he places his right hand on the desk for a moment beside mine. I stare at that familiar hand and I lay down my pen. I never touch him but I do now: I put my own hand on his, just briefly, and feel its warmth and press the trembling out of it, just for a second, and then I remove it and he passes on down the row.

He stands for a bit at the back of our row (I look around and see him there) and then the next time I look, he is gone.

The following day, I write him a short letter and he answers at once, in one line: "Thank you for your sympathy, and your love." He signs it "Hugh."

※

My marriage is arranged for the end of the summer, August 26. I unconsciously use a passive construction for the thought and then see why: things have gone out of my control. Still, I have all of June, July, and almost all of August during which time I can continue as myself. The wedding has to happen is what I feel, and all the time I know also that it is a bad thing I am doing, submitting myself to Frank's insistence or to some sense of fear. My relationship with him feels like something not connected to me. I can see this, and I know others can too, but no one steps forward to help me. My friends think they understand it and that I am in love with him. My father finally simply gives in: he cannot hold out any more about it. Even when Mr. Virgin comes bravely to call on my parents to lay out why the marriage must not go forward, Mr. Virgin being the only older person who has taken the time and interest to get to know Frank and is fond of him, they feel powerless in the face of my long-legendary will.

In a certain way my friends are right: I am "in love with him" but it is the way one can be in love with danger in a dream, excited by a wild joy in sheer destructiveness. And one wakes from such a dream in dismay for having dreamed such a thing. It is physical. I am physically excited by the look and feel of him. He is handsome and he is intelligent. He is athletic: I like all those things. His being part of the whole European romance for me, and part of all the suffering of war which loomed in the background of my childhood, those things are compelling. But I sometimes am shocked by his eyes. It seems as if he hates that he needs me so much. I sense he will have to hurt me.

He comes out to North Hatley from Montreal every weekend and we have yet another skirmish in the battle that has raged for three years: I will not offer up my virginity to him until we are married. I am giving him everything but that.

He clutches me to him in the boathouse, his face pressed into my neck. He actually cries with frustration and anger. He bangs his fist into the wall, painfully; he shakes his hand and yelps. He does not hit me, but he presses his fingers bruisingly into my shoulders and shakes me violently and my head rolls from side to side. I can see his eyes glittering in the lights that cross the dark room every time a car passes along the road above. He looks wild and I realize he is drunk. I am afraid of him.

Another night we walk very swiftly down the steep hill from our house to the lake. The road is a black tunnel and we can't even see where we put our feet, and he yells up at the invisible treetops furious words in a language I don't know, but certainly the anger is meant for me and the words presumably for the gods above, calling down damnation upon me. I long for him to be gone, for Sunday night to come.

I tell myself over and over the claim that he himself has made, that he cannot help drinking now and it is entirely my fault in any case, as he must seek oblivion to escape from the torture I am putting him through. He will have no need or reason to drink once we are married. But his fury at my behaviour, at my unkind and unnecessary denial of him mounts. I am abnormal and cold. The drinking does not appear to help much as any sort of calming device; as far as I can tell it foments his rage. I dread the weekends.

And mysteriously, and almost as often as he is horrible, he will be tender, and promise to love me always and say I am his Anyusha and absolutely necessary to him, and he will kiss me gently. I can acknowledge my own longing for him, when he is not furious and punitive. I think I want him, physically, as much as he wants me, maybe more, as with him there's such a power principle involved as well. In the good moments, I almost forget the bad ones, and the reverse is also true.

I am rereading some of my books of earlier years. Doing so allows me the illusion of slipping back into a less hazardous time, when I imagined my future life as dramatic and heroic and full of dangers, but ones that I would successfully negotiate. I would meet them and I would triumph. In those years, I would read or daydream of anything at all, however extreme, and know without even bothering to articulate the thought, that I was safe in my own single bed under the window with my tree outside — when I turned out my lamp I would see its dark shape against the paler sky — and the summer air would flow in my open window and over my face and nothing could really ever harm me.

Oh, my single bed.

I am rereading *Kristin Lavransdatter*. A very long tale (it is over a thousand pages), it is the story of Kristin, who is her father's beloved and favourite child, and who, oh so weakly yet so completely understandably, gives in to her insistent lover, Erland. She does not even enjoy the act he forces upon her. "It was as though her whole body ached with wonder — that this ill thing was what was sung in all the songs." It is fourteenth-century Norway and so she can think in such evocative and haunting language. Through that joyless submission, she loses everything she had, and was, and is hurled into a new and desolate place, a lonely landscape. She is ridden with guilt for breaking her father's heart and carries the sad knowledge of doing so inside her forever. I do not think that this act that Frank is trying to force me to allow is an "ill thing." I want it too. But I am not sure of all the reasons why I will not succumb. It feels as if I will lose so much. But what do I mean? My power of choice, somehow. Just — my power.

I do not want my married life to be clouded and poisoned by guilt about a father as Kristin's was. My father has already had too many women in his family fall from grace, the first, or so I suspect, his mother, and then in his own generation, his sister. About his mother, he still says almost nothing, though about his sister, his bitterness and distaste are more open. But all the women in his family (though not my mother, who of course was not born a Coleman) "sinned" in this way. I don't take a moral stand about their doing so and in fact think they were probably quite brave, but I have been cast in the role of the "good girl" of the family and willy-nilly am caught in it. It has become too important and I have played into it myself, but now I can't bear to shake my parents' faith in me.

But I am also rereading my old favourite, *Jane Eyre*, first encountered when I was nine in an edition with pictures, black-and-white woodcuts, both ominous and thrilling. Young as I was, I was electrified by my first intimation of what passion was going to be, by the certainty that it waited ahead not just for Jane, but for me. Indeed I got from that novel a lightning strike of what sex itself would be like even though no sex act is described.

I still remember perfectly my wild surmise: I was in our Toronto house on a winter evening, the curtains not pulled across and snow falling against the windowpane, and I was curled up in one of the big wing chairs in our living room. From one second to the next I suddenly knew what love between a man and woman could be. And I was "imprinted": it has been Jane's love for Mr. Rochester that has informed for years, at least as much as the Russian novels, how I've shaped my life. Mr. MacLennan has been for a long time Mr. Rochester, but now, though in a different way, Frank has assumed the role. It is Frank who is pleading with me, as Mr. Rochester pleads with Jane. And her reason for refusing is mine too, and a deeper one than just not wanting to hurt my parents.

Jane knows that by giving in without marriage she will be undone. On first reading the book at nine, I certainly did not see what I do now, that she cannot possibly stay on at Thornfield as Mr. Rochester's mistress. If she does so, she will be entirely vulnerable and at his mercy. Her precious "self," which for her is all bound up with self-respect and integrity, will unravel and she will lose her moral clarity and power. I know the same thing is true for me. When Jane and Mr. Rochester finally do marry, they do so as equals. That may not be the case for me, and I will put off that eventuality as long as I can, in order to be myself at least until the wedding cancels me out. Which is a fearful way to see it but I do. I feel that this cancelling is all that can happen because the kind of girl I am — or was, maybe she's gone already if I can think this — isn't a possible kind.

I walk down the hill and through the village on my way to Emily's every morning (I am working for her again this summer as I wait for my end) and my mind is full of apprehension and confusion. How does Mr. MacLennan fit in to all this, if he does at all, I ask myself. A little bit, he overlaps with my father, as another older man who is certain to see what I am doing as mistaken, disappointing, downright alarming. Both he and my father are good men; that is an important similarity between them and from that base, neither of them would want any "bad" man to hurt someone young and vulnerable like me, a young girl walking into trouble, wilfully, foolishly. At the same time, neither of them is prepared to do anything effective to help me. There is a fatalistic acceptance of my going ahead with this, as I seem to be insisting I will do. And yet all the while I am scared underneath and I wonder

how they don't see that. I find it hard to understand. Or does
it almost smack of spite: "She will, will she? Well, let her see
what happens," they may be thinking.

And Mr. MacLennan no longer has a wife.

I have been in love with him for years and he likes that; I
know he does. The few times that our fingers have connected
– though when I played at Bathsheba, a little more than that:
he put my fingers to his lips – those few times have been
charged with potential dizzying drama as though the birds
might fall from the sky were one of us to continue a step
beyond and fully clasp the other's hand. That time in the water
nudges at my memory but won't unfold for me. Whatever happened on that occasion, as well as whatever it meant, is brack-
eted off somehow, I imagine for both of us, and is as if it never
took place. And there I go again doing what I've done before,
assuming the feelings work both ways. I have no proof that
they do. I have only the way he looks at me.

I do not want to risk losing him before I have to. Maybe
this is the reason that is closest to the truth. I am holding
Frank off because as soon as I give in to him, Mr. MacLennan
will no longer love me. I do not even question whether he sus-
pects that I have given in already, because I feel certain that he
knows I'm still his. My thoughts circle about all this and go
over the same ground again and again.

I will not give in. Not until I must.

The oddest aspect of my life right now, or what would seem the oddest to anyone else, as it feels quite natural to me, is that in this summer leading up to my marriage to another man, I see Mr. MacLennan constantly, far more than I ever have before.

While his wife was alive, our meetings were essentially left to chance or perhaps just had to appear to be. An entire evening together was out of the question. However, during the week now we spend many afternoons and most weekday evenings together, when Frank is in Montreal, and ever since my family has moved up the hill, which we did soon after I got back after graduation, we are even nearer to his house.

Last year my father bought the whole pasture and the forest and hillside above it and he has built a new house into which we moved this June. I loved the old house in its situation among the trees, just one level above the lake, but this new vantage point high above the valley and the sense of space around us are wonderful. It is a long, low house all on one level, which I find I like as I can lie in my bed with my window wide open to the summer night and the outdoors feels surprisingly nearer than when I was up a floor.

I think of this house as "our house" as if I am still going to be a member of the Coleman family, which I will no longer be when I marry and lose my name and become a wife.

The new lawn slopes down to meet a low drystone wall, and beyond that is the meadow, still full of wildflowers and dotted with small clumps of apple trees. There are no longer any cows or horses. The house is on the very spot where Mr. MacLennan and I sat years ago and had one of our first long conversations.

Walking down our new long driveway and through our big white gates which are always open, I am on Mr. MacLennan's road. Within a minute I can pass his house. Except I don't pass. In the late afternoon he is usually around the back where he has planted a rose garden and I go around to him. I step along on the flagstones he has set to make a path between the house and a big bank of ferns, as the grass here is lush and always damp from underground springs. I still feel daring doing this, coming into his private space after never being here while his wife was alive.

Behind his house, the hill rises steeply and is thickly forested, but there is a flat area right outside his back door where he has made a small lawn, and now also these two narrow beds where he has put in roses. They are formal roses, not the old-fashioned bush ones I actually prefer, but I am prepared to be appreciative of his choices and of the fastidiousness with which he cares for them. No single blade of grass or straying bit of meadow flora is tolerated and the edges of the beds are sliced ruler-straight.

He is kneeling there weeding as I come up and he sits back on his heels and looks up at me. The knees of his pants are muddy and he has earth under his nails. I can tell he is pleased to see me. For some weeks now he has been able to be pleased, and his face has lost that look of strain that it held for a while. He is certainly far from over his sadness but he is no longer shocked and as if always listening for her voice. He doesn't speak of her to me any more now than he ever did. That he is grieving is assumed between us, or assumed by me, but our relationship still is a separate thing, only about us, and she is outside it, even in death. I thought at first that his making the rose garden so meticulously perfect in every particular was something he was doing as a memorial to her but he hasn't said that and I wonder if he would want me to be part of it if that were the case. Perhaps it's just that it gives him something to do, in the face of death, that is so definitely on the side of life: he has plans for the garden's enlargement next year. Making it so perfect, when he is not a fussy man about how things look as a rule, must be satisfying too. He can control this patch of ground, at least for now while he is here.

"Anne! Sit down with me and look at this. And smell it." I sit down cross-legged beside him and lean forward to sniff the deep-crimson petals that have unfurled almost but not quite to their fullest since we checked this morning. The flower is at the loveliest point of its brief life. This is the bush whose blooming we have been anticipating most keenly, the one he thought we would like best.

"It's perfect," I say, and he smiles.

"When I am away next week," he says — he is going to Nova Scotia — "I want you to come every day and weed. Will you do that? I don't want the weeds to get ahead of us."

I promise to come daily. "Come in and let's have a drink," he says then, and we go in though his back door, he treading in with him a certain amount of mud, and he washes his hands in a careless way before getting out several oranges. I never want an alcoholic drink, maybe partly because of Frank's excesses in that direction but also because I never have got into the way of it, and the first time he asked me in like this, I said I liked orange juice, so this is what he does for me: he squeezes oranges. I would be happy with something simpler, even just a glass of water, but this is our routine, and I like watching him fuss over this small thing for me, when as far as I can tell he is only very sketchily domestic. My mother told of how one day in LeBarons' store, he insisted on telling her how to cook a frozen cod fillet by covering it with an undiluted tin of celery soup, a recent culinary discovery of his and one which made her laugh when she recounted his instructions to us. Not that I can cook myself. I don't know how to do anything beyond putting the already prepared roast in the oven while Mother is at church.

This lack in me worries me from time to time: do new brides just suddenly discover they can do these things, or will I be foiled by a kitchen stove as I once was by a sewing machine?

Mr. MacLennan hands me my juice and pours himself whiskey, adds not very much water to it, and we go through to his living room.

"I've been reading D.H. Lawrence's letters," I tell him, "and I'm interested that some are written to Bunny Garnett, and I've discovered that he's actually the son of Constance Garnett. Ages ago I used to wonder about her and yet I never looked her up. I remember that I was even going to ask you about her: I wanted to know how she accomplished what she did, learning Russian and doing those huge translations."

"They were extremely accomplished, some of the bluestocking women of that generation, and the next generation too, the Bloomsbury people."

"Yes, they were." I think about that Bloomsbury group, whom I've encountered in various people's letters and diaries. "But the women were the background, weren't they, in terms even of how they valued their work themselves, let alone how the men did? I bet Virginia Woolf didn't consider herself to be as important as E.M. Forster, or Maynard Keynes, for two examples."

"Well, I don't think she was! One has to face the truth."

"I suppose so." I am not sure what I really think of Virginia Woolf and don't feel in a strong enough position to defend her work, or her, as I've only read *Mrs. Dalloway* and *Between the Acts*; I like them, especially the latter, though something hazy in her style bothers me. But I am liking her diary, which I am reading in odd moments. In it, I can sense the ground under her feet more than I can in the novels: I tell Mr. MacLennan that and explain, "There's something in all that airy musing her people do, in her fiction. It's like a mass of cobwebs and it sort of gives me the feeling I could put my hand right through it. But her diary entries are different; they're sharp and real. You feel an actual, physical human woman wrote them."

I have kicked off my sandals and am sitting cross-legged on his sofa and he is in a wicker chair. He takes a drink and puts his glass on the floor. He looks quite relaxed, happy maybe, even. The room is typical of the living rooms in old North Hatley cottages, with faded, Quebec handwoven cushion covers, the smoky smell of last night's fire. A bit of chill in the air; it's a shaded house. Old books. A few stacked magazines, probably from other summers. It reminds me of our old house, before it was renovated. I like that.

"I don't think we'll find that the work of the women of that period stands up," Mr. MacLennan says. "Or not in the same way the men's will. What woman is in the category of Hemingway or Joyce? Even now, Woolf is fading, is she not? It's not that long since she died and yet who is reading her now? And Katherine Mansfield – she managed only short stories, nothing full-length. Just consider: were either of those women on any of your reading lists at McGill?"

His face has a look of amusement. He likes conversations when we do a bit of duelling, and he wins.

"No, of course they weren't! There were no women on any of my reading lists, but I wish now there had been." He openly smiles now, which is a bit irritating as I'm sure it arises out of pure male self-satisfaction. "I took it for granted at the time that there weren't, and yet when I think of Woolf, I feel I've missed something and I'd like to have studied her to see if I could get it."

"Well, they can't make courses out of what simply isn't there, Anne. The English literary tradition is a male one, with a very few exceptions. There was no female equivalent to Shakespeare, or Milton, or Wordsworth and you can't gainsay that fact. Though it doesn't mean there never will be." This last is a sop if I ever heard one.

I can't resist a hit back at him: "There weren't any Canadians either and so can we conclude, using the same logic, that there are none of consequence?"

"Touché."

He lets me win for now, and he leans back, his hands clasped behind his head. His hair is rumpled and he has a smear of earth on his forehead. The contrast of his being the professor, talking of writers, and at the same time being my friend again, pleases me. I am aware of his eyes on me as I sit watching a small pool of late-day sunlight that falls on the braided rug. There are moving leaf shadows in it. Then I look up and meet his glance. Neither of us says anything for a bit.

I almost tell him another interesting thing I've discovered in my perusal of diaries and letters – and then at the last moment realize I won't say it: Bunny Garnett married Virginia Woolf's niece, Angelica Bell, the interesting point for me being the huge difference in their ages, twenty-six years. That Mr. MacLennan is older than I am by not much more than that stops my tongue.

The situation with Bunny and Angelica was even more out of the question, though she didn't know it when she married him, and still doesn't perhaps. I've found this out in a round-about way: I met a woman whose husband's cousin is married to Ottoline Morrell's grandson – very convoluted – and of course that Morrell family knew all the Bloomsbury gossip. What I heard was that Bunny had been Angelica's real father's lover – that real father having been the homosexual Duncan Grant, and not Clive Bell, the father of Vanessa's other children – and then years later Bunny went on to marry his lover's daughter when she was only eighteen. No wonder Virginia's diaries are being abridged, at least for now, because likely all those interesting details would be in them, as well as many other scandalous things about people still alive. There may be shady secrets in my family but nothing as tangled as all that. But I really enjoy finding out these kinds of things that open little peepholes into the intricacy of other people's lives.

That makes me remember something I need to tell Mr. MacLennan. Though it's not a story of enjoyable intrigue; it's one I find profoundly disturbing: "Do you remember years ago I told you about a woman locked in a shed?"

"I do," he says, "and you were vexed with me because I questioned the story."

"Well, I've wanted to tell you what ended up happening to her, because I was perfectly right and she had been a prisoner for years."

"How could that be?" He looks shocked but still disbelieving and is sitting up straight now, giving me his piercing blue stare when his eyes seem to leap out a bit. "Even if she could have been there in the summer, she'd never have survived in an unheated shack over a winter. It can't possibly be true."

"Of course she couldn't be there in winter! He'd move her in the fall." I like shocking Mr. MacLennan, but still I shudder, minding as much as when I first heard of it, hating to think of those twice yearly movings, when in dead of night presumably, the poor thing would, oh so briefly, walk in the outdoors, smell fresh air, and then be shut in again. "He had to shift her though, because his house, which is where he kept her in winter, locked in a room, I guess, has people in and out in summer. He's a sort of odd-job mechanic for summer people. So he had to smuggle her out."

"So how was she finally discovered? I assume she's out now?" He is looking really horrified now. I've upset him with this story and probably especially for the fact that he hadn't taken me seriously in the first place.

"My dad got her out," I say. This part particularly troubles me because I should have told my dad right away about her and I didn't. I hadn't wanted yet another person not believing me, and yet I should have realized that my dad is someone like me, and is aware of the black possibilities in situations and people. "He had to break the door down."

"Good God, how dreadful. It's almost unbelievable. But what happened to her then?"

"Well, they took her away. She was crazy. Though don't you wonder about even that? Wonder if she was crazy in the first place, I mean? Because I'd be crazy if I had to be locked in the dark and knew it was forever."

"So she really was a Mrs. Rochester. I'm sorry I didn't believe you, Anne. We might have rescued her sooner. That's really an awful story." He shakes his head and his eyes are really troubled. He is more surprised than I am that such a thing could have happened, that it could be possible, even in our village. We are both distressed but he is amazed too. I don't know if that makes it worse or better for him.

"There are lots of terrible hidden corners in this village, and in the countryside around here," I say. "And I bet there are anywhere; it can't just be North Hatley. There's a Robert Frost poem — do you know it? — where the traveller, I guess Frost himself, comes across a remote farmhouse, and he stays for supper or maybe even the night, I forget, and he finds a room upstairs where someone has been caged. He describes the wooden bars, all worn from the person's hands." That poem gave me the horrors, probably because it's real and I've brushed close to things like it.

"It's ignorance," he says. "It's ignorance, and the fear that arises out of it that makes people do these things."

"There's such a gulf between groups of people though: the kind of people that it could happen to, and the kind of people it couldn't." But that's simply not so, I realize as I say it, however I might wish it to be. There is no such safety and people cannot count on the fact that members of their group will never be overtaken by calamity, and their lives never snatched out of their hands. Perhaps especially the women of any group are at risk.

And I, right now this summer, am steering directly towards hazard.

Virginia Woolf, for all her brilliance, or maybe because of it, went mad and was shut away for long stretches, her power taken from her, her writing forbidden. Moments ago I was thinking of how I am intrigued by the gossip and scandal of the Bloomsbury Group, how I enjoy finding out about their sexual entanglements and their nastiness about one another and their careless housekeeping. But underneath all that, for them too it was there, the quicksand waiting to swallow any vulnerable one of them. Virginia drowned herself, shoving stones into her pockets to ensure she sank. It was not an impulsive act: she could swim, and so she would have had to think her plan through, and sustain her conviction through all the time she was writing her note to Leonard, evading him, slipping quietly away, and finding the correct size and number of rocks. Katherine Mansfield too had a dreadfully sad end, dying in France, coughing out her lungs, abandoned by her selfish husband, wretched.

Those were creative women who broke new ground in their art and in the freedom of their lives — and those were their fates. But Anna Karenina and Madame Bovary, who followed where love led them, in the older style, fared no better: death under a train, death by poison.

I don't share these thoughts with Mr. MacLennan. For one thing, I am only just formulating them and groping towards what they may mean for me and my life, and for another, I don't want to hear again his theories about women's power and its dangers.

I've never told him about the other Mrs. Rochester in the village. Her case is different and I don't really think she requires rescuing, as by now quite a few people know about her and I suppose have concluded she is as well off here as she would be in some institution. No one is cruel to her, not now anyway. In recent years, she has been more carelessly imprisoned, and she not infrequently eludes her husband/ jailor and slips outside, which is why the fact of her existence is no longer a secret.

She is very fat and moves slowly in her fat-woman's waddle, avoiding the roads and taking the railroad tracks towards the village. She would be quite easy to catch, but I don't think anyone bothers to try. She just takes her little breaks from her captivity and then wanders back, in her own good time. She is a nuisance, though: she slips into cottages. Few people in North Hatley lock their doors, and a woman will enter her own living room at dusk to put on a lamp, and be startled by this Mrs. Rochester figure rising from where she has been sitting on a chair or a couch, quietly, all on her own. Without a word she will lumber heavily away.

She invariably leaves behind her a wet patch.

Sometimes she is out before dawn. Swimmers going down to a boathouse later in the morning will discover an even more unpleasant mess on a verandah or on a beach. "Oh, no! Drat that woman!" But no one does anything about her. What is there to do?

All these Mrs. Rochesters: the two here in North Hatley and those others, literary and historical, mad or near mad, they snag my thoughts and pull me a little way into their stories, or what I imagine their stories to be.

I know I will never descend into madness myself; that feels impossible. My mind is too clear, too solid, for craziness to tempt me as any sort of possibility, or escape. I am not wholly rational, however, or I would not be heading in the direction I am. It's as if my own impulses and motives have gone underground where I can't get at them. This inertia in the face of impending disaster: I can sense it's related to the area of my mind that I've been shutting off for ages. Something in my head closes now when I try to see.

There is a dream I've had several times now in slightly different forms: I am driving a car down the steep hill that descends into North Hatley by St. Barnabas Church and the Connaught Inn. I know the corner is right ahead of me and I must stop. Four roads come together here. I must take my foot off the accelerator and put it on the brake. I don't do it. I simply can't be bothered. In the other version of the dream, I am carrying a baby. It is slipping from my arms but I could easily clutch it and save it. I let it go.

And yet despite these warnings of disaster ahead, I think, insofar as I can be reasonable about it at all, that I will survive my descent into whatever doom I am approaching. I will be a visitor below only, as Dante was when he went down into Hell. I won't have a Virgil to guide and protect me though. My only protection will have to be my own sane and strong will. Of course I also see that being on the brink is a very different place than being right in there.

I dislike obvious symbols in literature – my recurring dream would be too obvious, for example, in a novel. I don't like signposts that I sense have been placed by an author like tricks or traps in a landscape, providing a kind of coded map the reader is meant, eventually and if clever enough, to decipher. Something quite else happens when I catch in a text a flicker of something that was swimming deep in an author's subconscious and that signals to mine. It is like a fish I see out of the corner of my eye. I don't want to hook and land it. I want it alive and mysterious, and I just want to think about it, inconclusively. Thus far, these madwomen are like that. They are their own sad selves, sick and lost, and probably at bottom quite ordinary. But what has happened to them resonates for me in ways that perhaps some day I will understand. Or maybe I never will. Maybe all that matters is that I think about them. As for my dream, I realize that it's only obvious up to a point: it flashes to me a warning. It doesn't offer any hint as to how to step on the brake or grasp that baby.

Every afternoon I swim and while I am swimming, all my perplexities are in abeyance. I give myself to the water and think of nothing as I stroke far out and then turn and head up the lake. I love being out in the middle, with the great silvery and sleek expanse of water on every side of me, and I am lost in the rhythm of my movement. Every day I go farther.

When I get home, I play the piano, just now Bach's Two-and Three-Part Inventions, and the mathematical patterns I follow create a sense of order that calms me and seems to say all will be well, that my life also will play out like this, each note falling into its correct position.

However, when I am not swimming or playing Bach, I know that is not true.

While Mr. MacLennan is away I tend his roses as he asked me to, going early in the morning on my way to Emily's, and then I lie for a few minutes on the grass beside the rosebed and stare up at the trees. It occurs to me that what I want is for Mr. MacLennan to save me. Years ago, one time when he sensed I was upset, he said that he would always be on my side. I try to remember exactly what he said after that and I can't.

He is only away for a week. There is still a long stretch of summer left before I will be snatched behind that curtain.

I am frightened of the man I am marrying. His moods swing so. I never know who he will be, each Friday when he arrives from Montreal, until I see his face as he steps off the train: it is open, and smiling, in which case I smile back and hug him and slip my hands under his shirt to enjoy the firm, strong warmth of him, and we walk to the car (my dad's car, driven by me) holding hands, and I tell myself I am happy. Or he stalks along the platform with thundercloud face, his

mouth pulled down in a grim line and his eyes narrowed, and
if I try to touch him, he snatches his hand away.

Back in the winter, when I was still at McGill, my father
did react to the relationship angrily once. That first summer
when Frank and I had gone about together, my parents had
chosen to believe it would be a brief romance. It didn't turn
out to be. The next summer my father sent me to Europe.
That didn't work. Then last year Frank lost his job, and my
father arranged one for him that he could not afford to refuse,
a "favour" that suited my father's own purposes. Frank was to
be principal of a small school in a remote mining community,
and of course before the winter was over, he insisted I go up
for a long weekend. It was a long adventure, by train and by
bus and finally by taxi (I liked the driver's name, Joe Stocking)
along a narrow icy road through the northern Quebec winter
forest, endless miles with no human habitation, just the pines,
nearly buried in snow. Well, my father tried to phone me at my
McGill residence (such bad luck – he seldom phoned) and
was incredulous and wild at learning I had been allowed to do
this feckless, immoral thing. One of the companies he headed
was called Prospectors' Airways. Thus, after he got nowhere
sending messages over the radio phone – relayed into the little
general store to the village's delight, no doubt – he had one
northern bush pilot after another come and pound on the
door of the schoolhouse, where I visited Frank during the day,
or the Rectory where I was sleeping: "Anne Coleman must go

home at once." I never expect to be so famous in a community again, or so embarrassed. But I had no means to leave earlier than my original plan.

That was actually the only time I can ever remember my father being openly angry at me and, after the one explosion, he gave up fighting the situation. For some time he simply didn't speak of Frank, or to Frank, who gave up the job in the north as soon as he found another in Montreal in the spring. After graduation, when I told my father I wanted to be married this summer, he sighed. His expression made me sorry — for him, for me, too.

But I am confused by him: Why can he not speak of it in a way that would allow us to discuss it? His brief anger, and then his return to silence on the subject, are no help to me. His upset wasn't even at the genuinely alarming element in Frank. He was reacting to the "what will people think" aspect of my visiting a man. Now, he is polite to Frank but never really talks to him. Neither does my mother. On the weekends, Frank stays sometimes with the Virgins, sometimes with some other friends.

Emily and Mrs. Virgin have planned a shower for me. I have not thought of myself as having the sort of "normal" marriage that is preceded by such things, but then, even my mother's selecting my wedding dress seems to have nothing to do with me. They have arranged the shower outside on the lawn of the other member of the trio of women friends who have known each other forever, Anne MacKay (who was at

McGill with Emily long ago). She and her husband own the Connaught Inn, which is in the centre of the village and directly opposite the Flying Shuffle, so she is often in and out during the day when Emily and I are working and I know her well. She lives in a small house down past the Club and that is where we have the shower. Various friends of mine come, and my mother and my aunt, all women — which maybe is always the case at showers but I seem not to be *au fait* with these rituals. It is a lunchtime party for which several people have brought delicious salads and we sit in deck chairs or on the grass to eat these and to drink lemonade. There is a lot of laughing.

Then the gifts — which I had almost forgotten were to be part of this — are produced. I receive dishtowels, a covered butter dish of cream-coloured china painted with a pink rose, some of the woven placemats from the Shuttle, a basket for bread. Emily and Mrs. Virgin give me a set of small tables that fit one within the other. The last item I am handed is from them all and is a tablecloth on which all the women have put their names, in fancy writing and many different colours, in some kind of paint that will withstand washing and it is very pretty. And as I stare at it, a vivid picture of a moment that lies ahead of me leaps before my eyes, even as I sit in my deck chair on Anne MacKay's lawn. I see — this cloth on a table, and myself placing dishes upon it. The butter dish is there, with butter on it, and there is the basket of bread — and I am a married woman. I feel a wave of dismay.

It is a week later and I am walking down our wet driveway to Mr. MacLennan's. It has been raining all day though has now eased somewhat, but the trees are dripping and there are shallow puddles every few steps. As I pass under the overhanging branches near our gate, drops fall from them and run down my neck under my collar. I don't mind. It is a warm and humid evening and the water trickling down my back cools my hot skin. Mr. MacLennan has the records of the *St. Matthew Passion* and he has invited me down to listen. He knows I have the Mass in B Minor myself but this is his favourite Bach and he wants me to share it. We have not until now had an evening at his house. Always before we have gone for drives or walks, usually driving first, then walking, so as to be away from the village. It feels different arriving here as dusk is starting to gather. Looking through his screened verandah, I see the lamp is on, inside his living room, on the table beside the sofa. The shade is old and makes the light a dark yellow and it does not illuminate much of the room. I don't see him at first and the room looks like a stage-set, ready for something intimate to unfold, something very separate from ordinary life. Then he speaks my name and I realize he has been waiting in the shadows on the verandah.

It is such a strange evening; I don't know that I've ever had such a strange one. Listening to something so long, and doing just this one thing, this careful listening, and two of us doing it, so different from being alone with music, or, on the other hand, at a concert, creates a concentration of feeling that is far more intense than when we talk.

He is sitting very near me. I am in a white wicker chair in which I can lean back against a large pillow; he is in its mate, right beside me. A lot of the time his head is right back and his eyes are closed. After a while I realize that I am so aware of him, the way he breathes and sometimes sighs, once even groans, the way he shifts his position from time to time, recrosses his legs, folds his arms (his sleeves are rolled up on this warm evening) that I am not in fact hearing the music.

I consciously return my attention to it and close my own eyes. But that is worse. I have the image of him, how he is lying back in his chair. The image is sharper — especially the way emotions were moving across his face — closer somehow, than when I actually look at him. Which I open my eyes and do, again.

We do not speak at all even when he gets up to change the record, and as the highly emotive music goes heartbreakingly on and on — I am listening to it now — I want to cry.

I want Mr. MacLennan to save me. Badly I want that.

I watch his face in profile and it is full of sadness. I am sure he is thinking of his wife and not of me at all.

The music ends and the room is silent, except for the rain which has started again. I hear it dripping off the roof because the side window is open.

He stretches, stares at the ceiling for a moment, and then turns his head to me. He gives me one of those looks of his that seem to bore into me and which I can never interpret. They seem charged with something or other that he is on the brink of expressing, and then never does. This has happened so many times.

"Well," he says. "Well, Anne — there it is." And then: "I don't know what to do about you." He says this in such a low voice that I barely make it out.

If I were brave enough, I would get up and cross the little space between us and put my arms around him. I would press my cheek against his and plead with him to open his heart to me and I would open mine to him. But our roles have been in place for so long that I don't do that, even though his last words have created a tiny chink in the wall that separates us. I am not brave enough and I simply get up and stand there. I can't hold his gaze any longer now, and I look down at my feet in their new sandals, and I say, in the direction of the floor: "Thank you for the music. I loved it." Which is true, despite all the distress I felt while listening to it. And I look up again and smile and though he doesn't actually smile back, the mood in the room settles down.

As I walk up the road again through the wet, black night, I face the truth: it was up to me. It was up to me! He couldn't be the one to reach out, not with his sense of correctness. And — his sadness. I thought, he accepts being unhappy. He thinks he deserves it, even. But that's wrong. He doesn't. And I am a brave girl who could have shown him that. But didn't dare. I stand at the point where our driveway turns, just before I will see the lights of our library, and it is still entirely dark. I smell the moist earth and hear the stream, fuller because of the rain, rushing down through the woods that border our property, and ask myself over and over why I didn't cross that small distance and touch him.

I've heard people describe how when an accident is happening, time slows for you and it feels as if you should be able to reverse it, do something different, save yourself from the crash. But of course you can't, and it's really happening in a flash of time, a couple of seconds. This summer is not a flash of time – I'm having months! But I still can't move to alter what has been set in motion. On the weekends when Frank is loving, I breathe easily, and think, yes, it can be all right. And I reflect on a more hopeful aspect of my husband-to-be: I think about his parents and what strong and good people they are. Surely their son must have within him something of what they have, I tell myself. He must have some greater strength than I am seeing, as the son of those two people.

Two years ago, right after my second year at McGill, I spent the whole summer in Europe and while I was there I went to Yugoslavia. I stayed with Frank's parents for two weeks.

My father sent me to Europe for almost four months, and the plan was that I would travel about seeing the world, using as a base Geneva, where my oldest sister Ruth happened to be living with her husband. The unvoiced – but completely understood by both my father and me – rationale of the trip was that it was a lure or possibly even a bribe: a European trip and forget about Frank.

My poor father. His lure didn't work and while there, I became more certain even than I had been already that I must throw my lot in with a European. I was fascinated by the intricacy of Europe, the myriad strands of history playing beneath and upon the surface, the contrasts, the strangeness, the beauty, and the signs of recent suffering too. I was glad I had studied these countries, to understand at least a little of what I was seeing. The war had been over only ten years earlier and there were signs of it still. I travelled alone, mostly third class, which meant I was intently alert to everyone and everything around me.

In that summer of 1955, entering Yugoslavia had, right then, just become possible, though only a tiny number of tourists took advantage of the newly opened but still vigilantly guarded border. There was an omnipresent military, even in Bled. Walking around the lake one day, I strayed onto land that turned out to be Tito's summer estate and was immediately surrounded by machine-gun-carrying soldiers wearing

German-style helmets that came down over their necks. That
detail made their sudden materialization through the trees
even more threatening, as if I were thrown back in time to the
occupation. I was in a Koestler novel.

There was still a lot of fear around: my arrival at two a.m.
threw Frank's parents into terror. His ashen-faced mother
came bravely down the stairs of their villa, her long grey braid
hanging down her back. She was wearing just her long white
linen nightdress, such had been her haste to comply. A knock
at the door in the night usually meant one thing: prison for
someone, or, at least, interrogation.

Tinček, the old chauffeur, and Frank's childhood compan-
ion in mischief, brought me the last miles from the halt at
Lesce-Bled, scene of Frank's first encounter with the horrors
of war, that clutter of bodies on the road.

It was twenty-four hours since I had left Ruth's Geneva
apartment the previous midnight to board the Orient Express.
I had sat up all night as the train passed in darkness through the
Alps, and then, all the following day, stared out in fascination
at mile after mile of Italy. In the early evening we went through
Trieste, soon after which the guards surged onto the train to
check us before we crossed the border and entered Yugoslavia.
The train was almost empty by now, and I felt at moments
lonely and apprehensive, but mostly I felt adventurous. However, when I arrived at Ljubljana I realized that I had no idea
how to proceed. Trains pulled cattle cars into the station and

disgorged from them peasants carrying newspaper-wrapped parcels or bulging straw baskets. The peasants scrambled over the tracks as if fearful another train might run over them. I wasn't familiar with "peasants" in the flesh until then but recognized the genus at once. I was Anna, perhaps, before she enters her own first-class carriage where she will meet Vronski's mother. However there was no first-class carriage awaiting me.

The next thing that happened was extraordinarily improbable. I ventured into what looked as if it might be an information booth and the man there was young, spoke English, and knew who the Molnar family were. Later when I told Frank of this, he found it incredible: this was a large city, the capital of the province. Who this man was and how he came to know the family we never discovered. But this stranger was somehow able to tell me what to do, though he also revealed a problem: when I arrived at Lesce-Bled, I would still have a few miles to go and would be unlikely to find any conveyance there to carry me on, especially not at two in the morning.

However, there was nothing to do but hasten to the train, which was even now about to pull out. It was tiny and poorly lit, and the other passengers were some of the peasants I had just watched, or people just like them. Why they were travelling about in the middle of the night I couldn't begin to guess. Everything about the country was entirely strange and unreal, hardly a human world of the mid-twentieth century.

I started to worry. The train made frequent stops at which

one person or perhaps two would shuffle to the door and drop down into total, pitch-black darkness outside, even though there were no loudspeaker announcements and no apparent conductor. However, it turned out that someone was alert to me and finally a man appeared out of the gloom at the end of the car and gestured at me and to the door. I understood that now it was my turn to step off into the night. As I jumped down, I was at once conscious of a wild and frightening man who stood right outside, close to the train, an ogre or a demon of some sort, a creature out of a fairy story, his huge head of white hair catching such dim light as fell from the train door before it banged shut. Terrified, I moved farther on into the solid blackness, and then stopped. I was afraid I'd trip on something and fall, and had to wait a bit for my eyes to adjust and reveal something to me.

Well, the hairy man was Tinček, the first of the characters from Frank's tale I encountered and he was a good fairy not a bad one. Under the new dispensation, he drove a taxi. He took me safely to the villa and in the little bit of English which he quite surprisingly possessed, was able to tell me that he was growing his hair for as long as the Communists remained in power; it was his statement of individuality and protest. I discovered later that the inside of his taxi, which was the sole car in the village and ancient, was lined with cut up Persian rugs, though what that was a statement of, I'm not sure. Perhaps it was a way of keeping the rugs out of Communist hands.

That he was there so fortuitously, in the middle of the night when he could not have anticipated any business — as had the young man in Ljubljana been there against all reason — added to my sense that I was moving about in some sort of narrative. I was ushered to safety by improbable, chance-met strangers just as a girl in a fairy tale might be.

And so I met everyone: Jula and Sasha, Frank's parents, she with no English, he with a whole set of copybook phrases; Tončka, the old nanny; Aunt Mitzka. Sasha took me one day around the Grand Hotel, as Jula could never bear to return there; she found it too anguishing to see what she had created now in other, thoughtless hands and almost empty of guests, everything she had made there in disarray. After the nationalizing of the Hotel, the couple had been given a villa up the hill a short walk from the village, and to anyone not accustomed to life on a much grander scale, it would have appeared to be a pleasant place, quite large. They even had a servant. However to them it was a terrible descent.

To me, the despised villa, with its huge green, ceramic stove in the main room, the like of which I'd never seen, the lovely old carved furniture, the Persian rugs they still somehow managed to own, the delicious summer meals (vegetables new to me were served, peas in the pod my favourite), and the Turkish coffee poured from its little copper pot into tiny handleless cups — all these things were exotic and appealing. Sasha

took me on expeditions about the district in a horse and cart
and that in itself charmed me. And the village and its sur-
rounding countryside – woods and farms, the snowy mountains in the distance – were the most enchantingly beautiful I
had ever seen. I was ravished by it all, and by all the stories that
I learned of the family's history, both long ago and more
recent. I was shown many pictures of the old days, of Frank at
every stage of his life, and of all the ancestors. The Vovks
(Jula's family) had been free farmers here since the fourteenth
century, a matter of considerable pride.

How they survived economically was Jula's achievement,
though Sasha helped her. Improbably for people who had once
had so much, they made dolls. If this felt a humble occupation
to a woman who had ruled over a large and complex enterprise
and welcomed the grand and titled to her doors, she displayed
no sort of chagrin and was quite matter-of-fact about what
she now did. She worked long hours, breaking only for meals
during the day, and even sat at her table into the night making
her tiny stitches, fashioning with meticulous care these perfect
little people. Sasha undertook the simpler task of carving the
wooden figures; Jula dressed them. The dolls were made in
pairs and were dressed in precise, perfect renderings of the
Slovenian national costume. The woman wore the tall, pleated
headdress and a full dark skirt over which hung her chatelaine.
She had a minute lace handkerchief clasped in her hand. Even

more amazing to me was the man: he wore tiny boots of finest black leather high to his knees, suede pants, and a jacket hanging dashingly from his shoulder. In his hand he held a red, furled umbrella. Both man and woman wore what must have been the trickiest of all to create, an embroidered waistcoat exactly like something made by the mice in "The Tailor of Gloucester." I gathered that these figures were sought after and sold for a goodly sum as indeed they ought to have been.

Both Jula and Sasha assumed there was a serious relationship between me and their son: I felt their willing a marriage between us with all the force they could muster, and this was conveyed even though we were able to converse in only an extremely limited way. The language difficulty made anything that was said particularly significant. Meaning was pared down to the essential, as in a telegram or a headline.

Sasha did ask me one day while we were out walking if Frank was drinking too much. I did not answer, partly because at that point I didn't really know what "too much" meant but also because I couldn't bear to look too closely. Already my future with him was settled, whatever I thought or felt. Being there in Bled strengthened his claim on me considerably.

What Frank holds over me is his threat to use his Bosnian dagger, on himself not me. He will use it if I leave him, if I change my mind, if I will not marry him.

This is an old knife, its blade about six inches long, and the handle is made of bone. Grey with age, it is intricately, geometrically, carved with narrow lines of tiny triangles – a pattern I saw in Yugoslavia incised into many artifacts. It is quite a dull knife, and using it to commit suicide would involve a real job of sharpening before the deed could be accomplished, but Frank likes sharpening knives. It is one of the two domestic things he likes to do, the other being polishing shoes.

The threat makes me angry and I know it is both immoral and weak of him to make it. I cannot be certain how genuinely he means it. Maybe he really does. Perhaps if I told someone else about it, my dad, say, or Mr. MacLennan, they might be horrified enough to step in and extricate me from the situation, but I don't tell them. I don't know for sure why but part of it is that I am ashamed of having let myself be entangled with a person who could behave like this. Another thing is that, in a horrible way, having his life in my hands gives me a feeling of power. And that implies that I don't love him. Or maybe it implies the opposite.

I deliberately call up my memories of Jula and Sasha, how I liked their intelligence, their humour and their resilience. Jula's resourcefulness and hard work were impressive. They would be good grandparents of my children. Their son must, at bottom, be like them, I tell myself.

And Frank and I still do talk, when he is in his mild mood. We discuss his work – he is doing research now – and our reading. Over the time I have known him, he has made me read other books than I would have otherwise. Rebecca West's *Black Lamb and Grey Falcon* is important to me now too, and her dramatic view of the Southern Slavs, their qualities of endurance and tribal loyalty, their warrior history, colours mine. She found them enormously attractive. And Axel Munthe: we read him together also, and biographies of Galileo and other scientists that sparked Frank's boyhood interest. But the wedding approaching has made things feel grim. We seldom laugh. I'm not sure how much this is me, how much him.

Many evenings this summer, Mr. MacLennan and I go driving. We set out with no destination, just going up out of the valley and along one or other of the back roads, some of which I've never explored before because we go well beyond where I have hiked or skied. On warm evenings, we have the windows wide open and we are moving so slowly that the air in the car is almost still. Often when we see a field we like, often a long sloping one rising up to a line of maples along the skyline, we get out and walk. We talk or we are silent.

My parents think I am mostly walking by myself, though sometimes I tell them I have gone with him. They knew about the evening we listened to the Passion. They don't question me. They know he was my professor and that I admire him, but they have never, as far as I've ever sensed, thought there was any more to it.

One place we go to frequently is the Yellow House and I have been to it many times ever since I was old enough to explore. It is a favourite place of mine but the first time we went Mr. MacLennan was hesitant. Were we trespassing? I convinced him it was all right (I actually feel the place belongs to me in that I'm the person who loves it most) and he succumbed to its charms. There is a long driveway in and we leave the car up at the road and walk along the curving drive under the trees, until suddenly we are there, and we step out onto the wide lawn. The lake is to our left, below us, and the house lies ahead, its colour a perfect pale yellow – I want to have a house that colour one day. There are walled gardens and a rose garden – much larger than Mr. MacLennan's new little one – and trellises creating secret places. All the windows of the house are boarded up.

No one has lived in the Yellow House for many years. Never in my lifetime have there been lights in the windows, or people on the verandah that runs all along the front and around the corner on the west side. But every few days an old gardener arrives in his rowboat and tends the grounds. It's a long pull from the village and I often see him rowing by our boathouse, slowly bending and straightening over his oars, an oddly anonymous, timeless figure. When Carol and I were younger, we spent a lot of time at the Yellow House, exploring everywhere, rolling down the lawn, trying to peek in the windows, imagining we lived there. The house is set back on a point of land, facing the lake, and there is a tiny sandy bay with a boathouse where the gardener pulls up his boat, and where Carol and I beached ours long ago.

The house is owned by Mrs. Virgin's brother and while she is very committed to North Hatley and comes every summer, the never-seen Octave chooses to remain always in New York. And yet he won't sell the house: my dad tried to buy it once and his offer was scorned.

When Mr. MacLennan and I arrive, the gardener has always long gone home and we have the place to ourselves. There is something that satisfies me deeply in being here with him in a setting I have always known and one which, even so, has always seemed a little magic and strange, yet not "haunted," because it feels a happy house. Sometimes we sit on the verandah. There are no chairs of course so we sit on the edge and each lean against a pillar. More often, we wander down to the lake.

The lake is considerably wider than it is at our boathouse and the distant shore is mostly wooded, with here and there a cottage almost hidden among the trees. We sit on the grass as darkness gathers in the woods that border the lawn and the individual trees mass into blocks of shadow even while the sky still holds light.

One evening I tell him about Patsy's father. Up until now, I haven't told anyone but Carol, but suddenly I need to tell him. Twilight is thickening as I am talking, and I see a light come on way across the water, and then another.

He listens to me in silence, sitting there with his face turned away from me. I am aware of tension in his body. And then, as soon as I have finished — he leaps to his feet.

I stand up too.

He is horrified and upset way beyond what I expected.

I think I did want to shock him a bit; that must have been part of the reason I told him. But his reaction is far more extreme than I could have anticipated.

He starts abruptly to pace back and forth. He even clutches at his hair, pulling on it, a gesture I never thought to see though I've read of it, until it stands up around his head and he looks wild.

I feel dismay. Also in a way pleased.

He is muttering something and it seems to be Biblical. He is great for quoting the Bible, often at length. I hear snatches: "even unto the least of these thy creatures," and there is more along the same lines that I don't quite catch, some of which may even be in Latin.

And then he comes back to where I am still standing and for the very first time, he puts his arms right around me and holds me to him.

My face is pressed into his shirt and I can feel his heart thumping.

"Oh, Anne," he says, "Oh my God, Anne."

The strange thing is that it's been far worse for him to hear of it than it ever was for me to experience it. But having his arms around me makes having had those horrible clutchings and gropings worth it. Not that I had had any choice on those occasions, but I would have thought it a good bargain, if I had.

For a second I feel his mouth against my temple. It is not really a kiss, just his lips there. I feel the warmth of his breath in my hair and I have my arms around his waist as I did long ago in the lake, only this is different.

And then he drops his arms and pulls away from me. It is very nearly dark now but I see his expression.

"Are you angry with me?" I ask, because that's how he looks, angry.

"No." But he turns and walks a little way up the lawn, and then he stops and waits for me. "Of course I'm not angry. Or certainly not at you." And he walks beside me up the slope towards the driveway, and just as we reach the gravel, he puts one arm around my shoulders in a sideways hug, a different kind of hug, just a friendly one, and then drops it again.

His face is sad now and the anger I thought I saw has gone

out of it. I can tell though that he is still very upset and that it is a more complicated matter than being just to do with Patsy's father. His restraint cracked open for a little time back there and something leapt out.

I think I know what it was but I cannot be sure.

Ɂo

Ruth and her family live too far away to come, but in early August, Carol arrives with her babies and the unnatural quiet of the house — it has been the quiet of resignation — is broken. Both the house and the garden are overtaken by the children, their sounds, their clothes, and their toys. Teddy is two, not talking yet but understanding everything and full of dimpled smiles; Robert is one, plump and happy, almost the same size as his brother and walking sturdily about. They both spend a lot of time rolling down the lawn. They are beautiful children, dark-eyed and dark-haired like Carol's husband, and when I have one of them on my knee or am changing a diaper, I lean over to press my face into a baby neck and smell baby smell and am shaken by the strength of my yearning to be doing the same with my own baby. I vow that I will be, by next summer, and I can scarcely wait. A baby will be something that will make this marriage worth it and once I have a baby, I will not be alone.

Carol enters into the wedding plans as if what is going forward is the most natural thing in the world, no longer bringing up the earlier misgivings she'd had about Frank and had been unable to resist voicing at least once. She has always been a good actress so I cannot be sure to what degree her worry still lingers, but I suspect it may be stronger than ever. It was last summer when we had one huge row about it, as bad as any of our passionate fallings-out long ago when we were children, when our shouts and slammed doors could set the whole household on its ear. Those old fights arose out of some game that had gone off the rails, and after stamping about, we would make up, the air cleared by our noise. This time, the air didn't clear so simply and the trouble just went underground.

The row happened when she revealed to me that she and Uncle Bunny had been discussing Frank and me and the unsuitability of our relationship. Uncle Bunny is our dad's brother, younger than he by five years and a more open sort of man. He is far more approachable by his children than our father is by his and they discuss problems with him that we wouldn't dream of discussing with either of our parents, and I dare say he was, and likely still is, mystified by how I am being allowed to go forward with this thing I am set on without its being really thrashed out by my family. Of course I am glad, on one level, that my parents leave me alone to the extent they do, but sometimes I wish they didn't. I can't help thinking that Uncle Bunny's reaction would be more natural. Even more caring.

What Uncle Bunny said and Carol repeated was that Frank was an adventurer, an enraging accusation that I discounted immediately and loudly. It had such an old-fashioned ring too, smacking of the days of heiresses being seduced by phony "Barons" and "Counts" and subsequently milked of their fortunes. Even at the time I was reacting so furiously, I wondered just how near the mark it might possibly be. Frank can't think that I am bringing a fortune with me into the marriage, I told myself, but still it was a troubling thought. Now I am sure that it isn't anything so simple or discreditable. His parents welcomed someone like me as a wife for him, and his impulse likely is similar to theirs: he clutches at me out of an instinct for self-preservation, hoping that I may save him from himself.

Above all when hearing of my uncle's accusation, I hated the hot shame that overwhelmed me at having been discussed. So now Carol is silent on the subject though certainly not silent about anything else. We talk about every aspect of her marriage and of motherhood. She will be my matron of honour and we plan what she will wear, and who will restrain the little boys while she plays her part in the church.

Carol soon realizes how I spend my evenings and is intrigued, and by now my parents too have noticed how often Mr. MacLennan's car comes up our drive, returning me at the end of an evening. In irritation one day my father says, "Why is that man always hanging about our back door?"

Aside from that one remark, my parents continue to be quite astonishingly respectful of my privacy and I can't understand how they sustain this distance. And it doesn't feel like respect, anyway. It's something more lonely. They can't talk to me, nor I to them. It feels like abandonment, as if they have snipped me loose.

xo

"Anne," Mr. MacLennan calls to me from his porch one day as I pass by on my way home from working at Emily's. I walk over and look up to where he stands behind the screen. "Come by later," he says. "There's something I want to talk to you about."

I haven't seen him for a few days, what with the weekend and Frank being out from Montreal and Carol being here and all the planning that is happening. "Sure," I say. "I'll come down after supper."

I wonder what this is about and why he looks so serious. It makes me worried.

After supper, I walk down to his house and he has obviously been watching for me, as he comes out at once before I even get to the screen door. We get into his car, and on this occasion for some reason he takes a different direction than we ever have, and we drive through the village and along the road on the opposite side of the lake, towards Massawippi.

"I've been wondering whether I should do this," he says, "and I've decided that I will. In thinking it over, I realized that I wish someone had spoken to me in this vein when I was young, and that decided me."

He is making whatever is coming sound important and my mind moves over possibilities. I feel building suspense, and yet it can't be what I, however irrationally, had hoped it might be as I walked down the hill to his house, or he wouldn't be relating it to his own young self.

We drive on a little farther and then he pulls over into a spot where there is a gap in a hedge and a gated entry into a field. We both get out and walk over to lean on the gate and look down at the lake, which is a mile or so below us. The sun is still shining here, though the opposite side, our side, is in shadow already. As the late-day sunlight falls directly on him, I see some grey in his hair that I haven't noticed before. He is fifty now, I think. And I am twenty-one.

He takes out a cigarette and fits it into his holder, lights it. "It's important what I'm going to say: I have a sense of your future, Anne," he starts. "And I want to tell you what I see." A pause. "I'm talking about your future as a creative person." Another pause. "I think you are someone who will do something truly remarkable. I can't be sure what it will be, though I know you want to write, and it may be that, or it may be something else." He is looking outward at the view before us not at me and now I am doing the same.

He continues, "In my opinion, you have enormous potential and you will succeed at whatever you do, provided you pour your energy into it unreservedly. Matthew Arnold, as I'm sure you'll remember, spoke of genius being energy. I don't suppose it's really as straightforward as that, nor do I know if you have what the world would call genius, but you have great energy, Anne. It staggers me often, my sense of that in you. And intelligence, you have that too."

He pauses and turns to look at me and his eyes are so full of a kind of almost angry concern for me I am struck dumb and just stand there staring at him. He has spoken in a hugely significant way, as if he were for a moment an oracle, and has been vouchsafed eyes with which to pierce the veil that hides our futures from us. And my image of this veil he is piercing has nothing to do with the "black curtain" that has haunted me this summer. He is looking far beyond anything so personal and immediate.

I knew he thought I was clever and that he likes my company and finds me interesting, often funny, but to learn that he has such a sweeping vision for me first stuns, then thrills me.

He definitely has changed his mind about what is good for me. I remember how he used to want to pull me down to earth if he thought I was floating too high in my estimation of myself, and how cross that made me. This is such a different approach that I am amazed at him. And at once I believe him. He is right and it is true – I will be astonishing. I will.

I look into his face and he is smiling now, the oracular mood has passed and he is pleased to have excited me with this prospect he has laid out before me. Then he goes on: "It may take time, Anne, and you must be patient and continue to work towards it, however challenging and discouraging it may feel at times. I have a sense that you will find being young hard and that your triumphs and your greatest happiness will not come until you are middle-aged."

This is less exhilarating news, that my days of glory are a long way off. I suspect that there is something else at work in this part of his message. I realize that he is identifying with me. My future is to be what he has hoped for his own, is still hoping for, I have no doubt. He sees us as the same.

He has said nothing about my immediate prospects, my marriage which is hurrying closer and closer.

"Anne," he says and his intensity is back and his eyes flare at me again. "I want you to remember this. Remember this moment. It is important that you not lose what you recognize is true. Anne!" It's as if he wants to shake me awake, or into some other way of being awake. "I am telling you that you are capable of something wonderful. Don't be impatient that it may not be at once, perhaps not for what may feel to you a long time –" he has picked up my dismay at being told I have decades to wait — "but trust what I am saying. It's there in you, that potential. I know it is."

I look into his face. His expression is so full of his conviction, so intent on me. I feel myself smile. I also blink away tears, but I don't care about them and still hold his gaze. He is rising above such details as my wedding, my marriage, and whatever its immediate aftermath may be, and he takes me with him. For a moment I see his vision for me. The arrow of his thought — I imagine a blade of thin and shining steel piercing the air — leaps over our heads. It flies far beyond my present strange passivity, and even my unspoken need for him, into some clear-skied future place where I will take up my power again. Surely, yes. Yes. He is right. His eyes gleam bright with his certainty and stare into mine.

All the way back, driving along the lake and through the village again, I have that warmth inside me as if I am breathing some new and different air, even as I am just looking out of the window, not speaking. I turn a couple of times to look at him, at his hands on the wheel, as I have done so often and he looks back at me, a quick glance. I am digesting what he has said. I am determined to be true to it. To his belief in me.

Later, lying in my bed, I go over and over his words. I believe them, and waves of excitement break over me as I stare at the pale window. I have pushed it wide open, and I can smell the newly cut grass, a scent that carries me back to childhood, and I am filled with energy as I hear the small rustlings of the night and watch the moon, which I can see riding high over the trees. It is very bright and when I get up and lean on the sill to look out, the shadows of the hedge are black in contrast to the grey of the drive. The world is much too full of expectancy for me ever to fall asleep. But I finally do.

When I wake, I remember what he said. It rushes back and for a moment is real and true. And then I think, Frank comes tomorrow. There is such a tangle in my head. What do I want? — I find I am trying to recapture that sense of life's possibility, trying to hold on to it, rather than simply having it. There is too much that must be undergone first.

Oh, Mr. MacLennan, I think. I almost speak his name into the empty morning. But that feels melodramatic, and also someone might hear me.

Xo

August is slipping by.

"I'm scared," I say to him one night.

We are walking along the Minton Road up the hill behind our property, where there is a long, flat stretch underneath overarching trees and I always feel that it must be like England just here. We pass the house of Mrs. Virgin's herdsman, after which there are no more houses though a few cows move towards the fence and watch us go by.

"Why are you scared?" He says it very quietly, almost as if he knows what I am going to say and dreads to hear it.

I finally come out with what I've longed to tell to someone all summer and have not, to anyone. He must have a pretty good idea of it, I think, knowing me as well as he does, but I've never put it directly into words to him. Of course it's possible that he has chosen not to let himself see it. And I simply don't know at all what he thinks of Frank, whom he's seen for three years now around the village and on the courts at the Club. I don't think they've ever had a conversation though and that in itself implies something deliberate. I've frequently wondered if he can know just from looking at Frank that I am heading into something dire, and I've concluded that if he has paid attention, if he has used his imagination, he can. Of course he can. Any fool could see it. Including me.

"I'm scared of my wedding," I say and I hear my voice rise as I complete the sentence and consciously control myself as I go on, but it's hard. I'm so frightened at what I'm saying, at myself for letting out of my mouth these words I've not spoken to anyone until now. They make it more true and inescapable. My heart thumps in my chest so that it's hard to push the words out past the agitation. It makes me breathless. "It feels like my doom." And I give him the image that has haunted me. "It feels as if I'm advancing towards a cliff and I'm going to fall over it. I can't stop what is going to happen. It's my doom." I can't help repeating the word "doom" because its dark sound seems to hold the weight of my dread. He must pay attention! I want to yell at him, "Listen! Listen!" I want to yell, "Save me!"

I make a sudden step ahead and in front of him, turning to face him so that he has to stop or run into me. I can't bear for him to just walk on and that I can't properly see his face. He does stop and we stand looking at each other. He heaves one of those great sighs of his.

"I know," he says. And he looks despairing. "I've known right along and I've not known what to say to you." He rubs his hands over his face.

And then he says in a voice that is harsh with upset and almost as if he might be close to crying: "I've lived too long in the Valley of the Shadow to be your answer, Anne. And that's the terrible truth." He puts his hands on my shoulders and shakes me gently and then pulls me against him. This is the second time he has hugged me and this time he is desperate too, but differently desperate from the last time, when I felt a powerful excitement in the air, as well as anger. This time it is entirely a sad hug and though I can't see his face I wonder if he might be, in fact, crying. We stand there in the road like this for a long time.

If only I could dare to assume equality with him, insist that we properly open up to each other. But I can't. What he has said is too final.

I hug him back, very hard, as if I wanted to hurt him (maybe I do), and then step away from him and look into his face. It is desolate. I don't think that's too strong a word to describe the way it looks and I cannot read anything that holds out any hope for me.

And then I feel huge fury at him for not daring: he is older, he should be the one. He has been the one with his grand vision of my future. I have always known even that he loves me, though he has never said as much, and mostly I don't acknowledge the fact even inwardly. He hated bitterly to hear of someone doing me harm. When I told him about Patsy's father he was wildly upset. And now? And now?

But he says nothing more.

Somehow, and without looking at each other, we walk back to where he has parked the car.

Two days later I get his wedding present, which he must have sent away for before I got so terrifically upset with him, though he would have packaged it up and put it into the mail after that. What exactly did he feel, I wonder, as he wrote the label and signed the card, and I can't imagine at first, and then I think that perhaps it's quite simple: he really does mean his good wishes. And maybe he also hopes that there is something in the beauty of the music that will speak to me and comfort me, for it is what he knew I wanted, the boxed set of the complete Brandenburg Concertos. And it is Bach, the favourite of us both. But I can't be comforted for the loss of him; and there is something else too. Deep inside me I must have harboured just a little flame of hope that he would act in the nick of time, and now that is quite blown out. I'm not sure of this but my sense of hopelessness has a finality to it. Or maybe it's just that the wedding is only days away.

We have no more of our evenings; I simply don't go down to him, and I see him only one more time before the event. We encounter each other in the Post Office one day and then he waits for me on the porch outside. "Anne," he says, as I come out to pass him, "I can't come to your wedding. I know I said yes but I can't; truly I can't."

I have to have him there, I realize. I can't bear it if he doesn't come. I stare at him.

"I need you to be there. Please, please be there." This time it is I who am almost crying all of a sudden. He must come or I can't go through with it is how I feel at this moment. And I can see by his face that he relents.

"Very well. If you insist on it."

On my wedding trip, I cry.

We drive south from North Hatley down across the border into Vermont and on to Maine. We are going to the sea. And my tears flow and they will not stop. It is upsetting for Frank, my new husband; he is increasingly distressed and finally of course angry. He always has ready access to rage, and even while I cannot stop crying, I can see that this is not the way a bride should be behaving.

Why am I crying? I hardly know all the reasons but they seem to be myriad in number and huge: I am leaving behind my parents, North Hatley, my girlhood. Principally, I have let go my handhold on safety, which has always rested on my own bold, clear, and separate self. I don't know who I am any more. I knew this was coming and that doesn't help a jot. I have faced the drop-off and now I am falling.

And there is Mr. MacLennan.

I keep seeing him in my mind, as I saw him then, at the wedding. I see him as if in a series of coloured slides.

He is his perfect, handsome self, still young-looking, his features so distinct, so familiar. He is wearing a beautifully tailored, pale grey suit that I have never seen before and his hair is newly cut so that I see the perfect shape of his proud head. He stands in the church and, later, he stands against the light of our big living-room window, and he is very – still. Throughout all of it, there is an intensity in the way he watches me. At one point he is sitting beside me on the piano bench.

"Well, Anne," he says very quietly, "you've done it."

His expression – always I have tried to read his expressions – is tender, I think, gentle.

It is so sad. That is what the stillness is about; it is sadness.

He came because I insisted. I realize now, driving south-wards away from everything, how much he must have called upon his long-hoarded stoic strength to come to my wedding. I made him come and he came.

That was how selfish I was.

❦

That stillness with which Mr. MacLennan watched me: I look back and I cannot be certain how consciously, or I guess I mean how analytically, I thought about him as Frank and I drove southwards — away, away from everything — or if I did at all, then.

It was those images of him standing and staring at me, and the sound of his quiet voice as we sat on the piano bench, that recurred over and over in my mind. And they did so for days. They were so imprinted upon me I can still summon them up in total precision, and pain. Indeed when I try to remember details of my wedding day, I have no specific memory of anyone else — not Frank, not my parents, not even my sweet nephews, who must have been running and tumbling about our living room at the reception. But perhaps my thoughts were less coherent than I have described in putting myself back to that day and that drive. Could I have really been aware that it was anger I felt — and then that I did not feel it — all the while crying so steadily, for so many hours, those unquenchable tears?

I think it took me many years to recognize how much anger I felt then, and far longer to see that it should not have been at him, or not only at him.

The bond between us, once so compelling, broke that day. That has been my belief for all the years since, until now, when I realize that for me at least it just went somewhere deep underground. I used to see him every little while, each summer, and we would talk. His cottage, after all, was just down the hill from my family's house where I still spent every summer, for time had continued to move me forward, until it had carried me to that moment I'd had such a clear and surprising vision of long ago, when I saw myself fleeing across a field, with a baby under each arm.

Now when he first came out from Montreal in the spring, he would always have a long tale of woe to tell of all the illnesses and misadventures of the winter. He had turned very fast into someone else, a person I could not recognize, or could not bear to recognize. He did remarry and I hoped he found some happiness, but whenever I saw him he seemed deeply preoccupied with all that was grim and dark, whether on a personal level – the winter's toll on his health, a bizarre accident he had suffered – or provincially, nationally, globally. His distress exacerbated by alcohol, he seemed increasingly fearful and intolerant of the world around him. Listening to him filled me with a discomfort that was visceral and I couldn't wait to get away from him. If I saw him ahead of me along the road, I would avoid him by heading down the steep lane that descended through the trees. If he came out as I passed and hailed me, I was trapped. As fiercely as I had once loved him, I hated this new wilfully miserable man.

I had fled from my husband, and in my new freedom, I was restless with and had no time for the grimness that surrounded Mr. MacLennan, or for the sadness that had brought him to that place. Our old closeness seemed like something that had existed between two other people.

Only once did the person I had known emerge briefly from within his cloud of hypochondria and anxiety, and he seemed to know who I was, that I was Anne, and that we had once mattered to each other.

It was the middle of a summer morning and we met on the road near his house as I was walking along on my way home from the village carrying some grocery bags. My children were with me but he didn't glance at them; indeed he had never really taken a good look at my children, and yet they were sturdy and beautiful and merited attention. Or so people generally felt on meeting them, struck by their clever dark eyes, their slender swiftness, and their slightly exotic look. But Paul and Jane didn't care either about this man they didn't know and they ran on to our gate.

He had been about to get into his car, but seeing me, did not. He stood facing me as the children raced away.

He looked straight at me and his eyes had some of their old spark, and he spoke my name with force, anger even. "Anne!"

And then there was one of his old silences as he just looked at me.

I looked back at his so different face. His features that had been so fine were blurred as if I were seeing them through a veil of water; his face had a puffiness, and a hectic redness. But his eyes — for a moment, I saw in them the man I once cared for, so much. "Mr. MacLennan," I said. "Good morning."

He paid no attention to that. He had something he needed to say: "My God, Anne, you were a truly horrible child."

For a moment I was thrown. I didn't know what he meant. He had not thought I was a horrible child. I knew that.

"You were a terrible child." He closed his eyes. "A terrifying child."

And then he stopped and looked at me again. "You were so . . . so . . . ."

I waited.

He didn't complete the sentence.

There were a few summers before he died when he no longer came out to North Hatley. His cottage had fallen upon hard times by then. He had long given up his old care for it and it stood there through all the harsh winters and the snow, and the hot summers and the rain, becoming more and more pathetic, needing paint, needing torn screens to be repaired. Gradually it sank almost to its knees in the long grass.

His lilies and his peonies always came back. I considered them mine and picked them. The roses had gone to briar long ago. I would stand sometimes behind the house, losing myself in memory, while some lilies I had gathered stained my white pants with their dark pollen.

I could see him there, sitting back on his heels, smiling up at me, proud of his roses. He is about to offer me a glass of orange juice.

After my terrified run with my babies, I found again my lost strength, the strength that I had let slip away from me. I realize that it was the very strength he had seen in me so long ago, when we stood in evening sunlight looking across to our side of the lake, and he foretold my future. In my freedom, I discovered the great joys of independence, of raising my children, and teaching. At a time when few women were starting down that path of independence, I never doubted that I could do it.

And now I am even, at last, finding myself in that clear-skied place of creativity he had envisaged for me. Curiously, it is only now, as I'm writing the closing of this book, that I am able to see that. For many years after that encounter on the road, I returned to North Hatley most summers, but we no longer sought each other out. I would see him — by his house, or in the village, or with his second wife at a cocktail party. We might speak a little, but never again did either of us seem to acknowledge the relationship we once had. For my part, the distancing had come about from my confused sense of shame, a tangle of shames. Shame for him, for the bitter and frightened man he seemed to have become, shame for myself, for my response to him. I had turned my back on him. At the time it felt instinctive, as uncomfortable actions can feel to be when we attempt to exonerate ourselves for them. Because of the sheer discomfort of facing that, I've not, until now, been willing to revisit in my mind, in detail, what happened between us over the course of those summers we were close, and to try to delve into its complexity. What I realize is that now, in a critical sense, in a long-term sense, he did save me. His belief in me, his sureness of my strength, my energy, my abilities, all of that lit something in me that made the way I have lived my life possible. Maybe even made this book possible.

But something disquieting still hovers, not entirely resolved. There are deeper aspects I haven't plumbed.

There is something here that I am groping for.

"I have lived too long in the Valley of the Shadow to be your answer." His words daunt me still with their finality. And somehow at last it is clear to me what I didn't fully see before: his narrowly focused response seems to mean only one thing. He could offer me nothing, if he could not be my "answer." No advice, no support. At that moment he was blind to any possibility of his other roles with me — as mentor, friend, father, even — coming into play. I think now that he did love me, more deeply, more as a man loves a woman, than I ever guessed. And his fearful inability to act on that specific love eclipsed everything else, any other way he might have helped me.

It is hubris, the old sin of pride, to imagine I could have had the power to save him. I didn't betray him. Fate itself did, the gods, making him old and me young, and both of us stoical. Or perhaps a better word is honourable. I cannot claim responsibility.

And yet I am guilty of it still, that hubris. In some corner of myself, I still think that love, my love anyway, should have had that power.

Swimming Back: An Afterword

I wrote this book in two months during the summer of 2002, fifty years after the events I describe. I was not by this time in North Hatley, the setting of my tale, but in Victoria, British Columbia; the swimming was not in fresh water but in salt; the rocks were prickly with barnacles. The writing of it became suddenly possible, indeed necessary, as chance strands came together for me.

Memory opens for me through my body. I slip back because I catch a smell, hear a sound, or hold an evocative flavour on my tongue. But these single-sense glimpses of or gusts from the past are often fleeting. More compelling for me, more total, is when my whole body, the entire surface of my skin, and my muscles' movements connect me to my old self. Especially it is the movements of summer, when more of me meets the elements, while I am swimming, or feeling my bramble-scratched legs against hot rocks. Or when I am experiencing the lovely lassitude that fills me at the end of a long afternoon of sun and water as I stand slicing tomatoes for my supper, while corn boils, and sun falls in the window on a pile of raspberries in a bowl. All my senses, all, are alive.

As part of a "memoir" about growing up in North Hatley, I wrote a chapter about my relationship with Hugh MacLennan. In that "memoir" I was attempting to discover just what underlay the myths that I had created for myself as a girl, and through which I understood the world (and still do). My beloved North Hatley was certainly a central element. I discovered that while life's changes had exiled me from the place as it now exists, the village and landscape of my girlhood were still alive in my memory and imagination. I started to draw them to the surface. My efforts to recapture the past circled inconclusively around my friendship with Hugh MacLennan. For years and years the fact of it still floated somewhere in a far corner of my mind, though it essentially had ended in 1957, the summer I turned twenty-one. He died thirty-three years later, in 1990, at the age of eighty-three. That is a long time for him to have been still in the world and for me never to resolve for myself what had really happened between us, and why whatever it was had stopped happening. And why the thought of him was painful to me. I knew he was important to me and to the person I became; I chose not to think about it. But having written about it, I became restless. Something was tugging at me. The chapter had pulled him closer, but there was more.

I then turned the chapter into an essay, making it its own thing, as if that might do. But it wouldn't satisfy. I'd still told the story from a distance, from the vantage point of myself now looking back. A writer-friend whose authority I was prepared to accept advised me to go back in time to tell it as if it were unfolding in the present. I wondered at the legitimacy of that: would it lead me too far into invention and away from the truth, which was what I wanted to discover, and was the entire point for me in the exercise? But the advice freed me. As I recreated him, Mr. MacLennan stepped forth, stood before me, spoke. And I inhabited my own young self. What I have written I suppose is "creative non-fiction." I have taken liberties, moved events about in time, elaborated upon or created conversations. It is truth I am after, the true narrative, but it has to be subjective. It is *my* truth I am after and, insofar as I can understand it, the truth about him. For that I had to go as deeply and honestly into my imagination and understanding as I could.

So that was luck: the right, perfectly simple advice coming at exactly the moment I could use it. Was hungry to use it, as it turned out. Once I began, I couldn't stop. The project consumed me, obsessed me, and I wrote swiftly. The door into the past stood open. I started by saying my body was the key, and it was. The pattern of that summer of 2002 was this: I would write all morning, and then my friend Karen and I would drive out of the city and up the Saanich Peninsula to a beach we had found that few people seemed to know about. Mostly we had it to ourselves. Sometimes a few young boys would be there too, but they would find a log to ride on and head out around the point. In any case they presented no threat to my unfolding process. They were part of the timelessness I had entered: there should always be water-slick children's bodies at a shore. All afternoon Karen and I would swim. It was a beach within a shallow bay which itself was within a much larger bay. Thus we had a wide view, and the sense of the vastness of the Pacific out there not too far away. At the same time, it was protected enough to be calm. We wanted to swim, not just jump about in waves. I hadn't swum so much so regularly since I was a young girl.

My girlhood summers were all about water, swimming in it, sailing on it, canoeing across it. And now I find there is something mythic about the movements of swimming, the mystery of dark, deep water beneath me, pleasantly scary (what might be down there?), and it is there at the level of my face, against my mouth, its sleekness, its silvery or blue or pewter or clouded green expanse. The sea has more of this of course, this sense of its being alive and its own strange self. It is moving and changing all the time, and the beach is never quite the same from one day to the next. But Lake Massawippi seemed as good as a sea to me, long ago. Magically, in my sixty-six-year-old body, I was, while swimming, the same person I was back then. I don't mean I'm deluding myself that I looked like a girl and not a grandmother, but all the sensations of water and sun and sand and rock, that summer they met my skin as they had long ago.

So I blurred the dividing line between now and long-ago. I started to write about myself back then, and about Mr. MacLennan (not "Hugh MacLennan," as in my essay version. Long ago, he was "Mr." It was part of his potency.) As I wrote, I increasingly realized that what I was uncovering was truth, not of every fact, perhaps, but the essence. I had no interest in exaggerating, in making what happened more dramatic than it was. Words that he spoke, which I had always remembered, came back in their context, the places where we sat or walked. The fierce and quiet emotions. His eyes.

And as well as the precisely freeing words and the mythic swimming, there was a third element in my good fortune: I had the perfect first reader, the perfect listener.

Karen Chapple and I have been friends for forty years. I have an image in my mind of the two of us as young women, how we would stride swiftly through the small town of Lennoxville, Quebec, and over the bridge to the university. We were both tall, with long hair worn in one long braid, hers corn colour, mine brown. We looked striking I think now. We looked quite terrific! I can say that at this distance surely, of those two girls (then, we were allowed in our twenties still to be girls) with their academic gowns floating out behind them, their straight backs, and the speed of their progress. And now, forty years after those swift walks, in the summer of 2002 we swam, breaststroking side by side. We talked. We let our childhoods and girlhoods float into the present.

Every few days, I would hand Karen my pages and she would read them. She can read in a double way, hearing as well as seeing the words. She would say, "Read that sentence aloud to me . . . and again" – and we would both listen. And she would sometimes say – "There's something there. Do you hear it?" There would be something awry in the cadence.

The place I was summoning back no longer exists. North Hatley nowadays is another world from the village I knew as a young girl. Then, it was many worlds, existing separately and almost entirely ignorant of each other, divided by class, language, education, even nationality.

Now it feels homogeneous. Its extremely pretty surface seems to be all there is. It has become quaint. There are hanging baskets on every side, boutiques, galleries, bed and breakfast establishments, world-class inns. Then, it had many dark corners, many mysteries. Beauty, too.

ACKNOWLEDGEMENTS

I am full of gratitude for the crucial help of my long-time friend Karen Chapple, for listening and reading with such sensitivity as I went along.

Thanks also to family and friends who read the manuscript and gave reactions: my daughter, Jane, my son, Paul, my granddaughter Sarah (and her sister, Rebeccah, who didn't have the chance to read the book but sent key advice by e-mail from Thailand), my sister Carol and my brother, Charles, my cousin Charlotte, Anita Galitzine, Cynthia Ross, Donnie Caverhill, Rachel Gardiner.

My editor, Ellen Seligman, helped me vitally with her patient, perceptive, sometimes humorous, always inspiring insistence that I "go deeper." "There's more," she would say, and I would realize that there was. Our three-hour telephone talks, with her in Toronto, me in Victoria, were challenging, exciting, also fun.

Others at McClelland & Stewart were important and helpful in the process: Douglas Gibson, who read the manuscript first, Anita Chong, Marilyn Biderman, Kong Njo, Jenny Bradshaw.